THE BOOK OF
SECONDS

Mark Mason is the king of trivia, those fascinating facts that slip down the back of life's sofa. He is also the author of *Mail Obsession: A Journey Round Britain by Postcode* and *Question Time: A Journey Round Britain's Quizzes.*

@WalkTheLinesLDN
www.theimportanceofbeingtrivial.com

Also by Mark Mason

The Importance of Being Trivial
Walk the Lines
Move Along Please
Mail Obsession
Question Time

THE BOOK OF
SECONDS

The Incredible Stories of the Ones
That Didn't (Quite) Win

MARK MASON

WEIDENFELD & NICOLSON

A W&N Paperback
First published in Great Britain in 2018
by Weidenfeld & Nicolson
This paperback edition published in 2020
by Weidenfeld & Nicolson,
an imprint of Orion Books Ltd

1 3 5 7 9 10 8 6 4 2

A CIP catalogue record for this book
is available from the British Library.

ISBN (Mass Market Paperback)   978 1 4746 0848 0
ISBN (eBook)   978 1 4746 0849 7

Typeset by Input Data Services Ltd, Somerset

Printed and bound in Great Britian by Clays Ltd, Elcograf S.p.A.

Weidenfeld & Nicolson

The Orion Publishing Group Ltd
Carmelite House
50 Victoria Embankment
London, EC4Y 0DZ
An Hachette UK Company
www.weidenfeldandnicolson.co.uk

PREFACE

'Winning is everything,' say those tiresome Americans, 'second is nowhere.' Well actually second can be thrilling, intriguing, heroic and pure. Luck and chance may have kept you from hearing of John Landy, Bud Rogan and 'You Better Run', but that doesn't mean they're not worth hearing about. They are respectively the second man to run a sub-four-minute mile, the second-tallest man in history and the second video played on MTV. You know the TV channel chose 'Video Killed the Radio Star' as a warning to the radio industry, but you didn't know they followed it up with Pat Benatar's song to underline the point.

For too long these seconds have wallowed in the shadow of their more famous firsts. It's time to hear how the second person to swim the Channel wore motorcycle goggles, how the second person in space ended up resenting a chimpanzee, how the second-tallest building in the world uses a clever design element to cope with high winds. And how the second team to conquer Mount Everest tested their equipment in a butcher's cold-storage room.

Sometimes definitions can be tricky. For instance the question of the world's longest (and therefore second-longest) river divides scientists. Top spot traditionally went to the Nile, with the Amazon just behind it. But in 2007 new definitions of both the Amazon's source and its mouth put the South American river ahead. (Another issue is the scale at which you measure – by zooming in and incorporating more bends you can increase the overall length.) And clearly we can't include matters of opinion, like John Gielgud's view on the bores of London. This came to light one day when he was lunching at the Ivy with the playwright Edward Knoblock, and someone they knew passed by. 'He's the second-biggest bore in London,' confided Gielgud. 'Who's the biggest?' asked Knoblock. 'Why, Edward Knoblock, of course,' replied Gielgud, before adding hurriedly: 'Not you, of course – the *other* Edward Knoblock.'

No, this book will deal with the clear-cut cases, the seconds who have definitely been robbed of glory. Like Margaret Wintringham, the second woman (after Nancy Astor) to take her seat as an MP – she used to bring her own enormous teapot to Women's Institute meetings as she disliked their urns. And the Tonga Trench, the second-deepest point in the world's oceans, where the male angler fish latches onto a female with his mouth and never lets go. And the clock faces of Liverpool's Royal Liver Building (the second-biggest in Britain), whose hands started moving at the exact moment George V was crowned.

So stand back, all you firsts – it's time for the seconds to emerge into the limelight and take their bow.

PEOPLE

---◆---

Bill Burgess: second person to swim the Channel

There are only a few weeks each year when the tides and sea temperature allow an attempt at swimming the Channel. The task is incredibly difficult, each 'as-the-crow-flies' mile requiring a much longer distance in the water. Even so, it's amazing that it took 36 years and 80 attempts before anyone could repeat Captain Matthew Webb's maiden success of 1875. Among those who tried were people by the names of Jabez Wolffe, Montague Holbein and Drugolloub vel Militchevich (a Serbian long-distance swimming champion). In the end the laurels went to someone from Rotherham called Bill Burgess.

Born in 1872, Burgess had learned to swim at the age of five during a holiday on the Isle of Man. He had to – his uncle had thrown him into the sea. When the family moved to London his talent was nurtured: as a youth he swam from Blackfriars Bridge to Battersea. Even a move to Paris, where he established his own business, didn't stop Burgess from swimming: he competed at the 1900 Olympics – for the French (this was then within the rules). He won a bronze medal as part of the home country's water polo team.

His father called Burgess 'a sane man on every subject but Channel swimming. That was the one bee in his bonnet.' He had failed 15 times to cross *la Manche* (as the French call the Channel – it means 'the sleeve', and describes the sea's shape). Then, on the morning of 5 September 1911, at the age of 39, after a hearty breakfast of ham and eggs, Burgess stepped into the sea at Dover and began swimming his 'overarm side stroke' (like the front crawl but with the right hand kept permanently in the water, pulling backwards as the left arm comes over). For this attempt Burgess had done only 18 hours' training, his longest swim a mere 6 miles.

His 6-foot, 15-stone body was smeared with lard, but 'owing to the hot sun, I was unable to put on more than one pound, instead of the usual three or four pounds'. This meant he was relatively unprotected from the cold water, as well as from the jellyfish which proceeded to sting him 'in large numbers'. Unlike Webb, Burgess wore goggles: motor-cycle goggles, to be precise, which started to leak, allowing the salt water to make his eyes smart. During the night the Moon at first came up, but then dimmed, and the big electric lamp on board his support boat failed, 'so we had to manage with the boat's lamp, good enough to steer by but not very cheerful'. A dense fog came down, and for a while the boat lost him. He also suffered heart problems, and had to hold his left hand over his chest to ease the pain. This obviously slowed his pace. 'I soon got very despondent,' said Burgess, 'and although awake, I had constantly before my eyes the vision of a body of a mutilated man.'

Food and drink were passed to him on the end of a pole: chicken, chocolate, hot milk and grapes, as well as tea to cure his indigestion. He also had 20 drops of champagne every hour, 'and not a drop more'. He asked his support team to sing to him in an attempt to raise his spirits. He liked their choice of the 'Marseillaise', but not the way they rendered it: 'They can't sing for sour apples.'

Eventually, 22 hours and 35 minutes after leaving England, he arrived at Cap Gris Nez in northern France. One of his colleagues, J. Weidman, jumped from the boat. 'I said to him: "Bill, put yer feet down." Gradually he got his feet down, stood upright, then staggered, and was about to fall. I caught him and helped him up the sandbank, and laid him down. He started crying like a child. This fair upset me, and I began to cry too.' Burgess was then wiped down. 'Having had a little champagne,' he said, 'I was soon myself again.'

Someone else who was pleased that Burgess had made it was Madeline, the widow of Captain Matthew Webb. (Webb himself had died in 1883, attempting to swim through the whirlpool rapids at the base of Niagara Falls – clearly dry land held little attraction for him.) Mrs Webb said how relieved she was that her husband's achievement had been repeated: it ended the suspicions held by some that he had not, in fact, made the crossing unaided.

In 1926 Bill Burgess trained Gertrude Ederle, the first woman to swim the Channel. The second was Amelia Gade Corson, later the same year. She had once swum the 42 miles around Manhattan, and made someone who bet on her swimming the Channel a profit of $100,000: he'd backed her at 20–1. Two men who made the attempt with her failed. Corson kept going by thinking of her young son and daughter: 'Their two dear faces were always in front of me.' Seven years later Ethel 'Sunny' Lowry became the first

British woman to swim the Channel, though she was called a 'harlot' for revealing her knees in the process.

Burgess was commemorated with a bust that stood in Rotherham's Main Street Baths, and was later moved to the town's Sheffield Road Baths. A light-hearted superstition arose that any schoolchild who failed to rub Burgess's nose with their towel before entering the pool would drown. So many of them played along with this joke that his nose eventually took on a distinctive shine.

Ruth Bader Ginsburg: second female Justice of the US Supreme Court

There are nine members of the US's highest court. The gender score had always been 9–0 until Sandra Day O'Connor joined their ranks in 1981. Twelve years later Ruth Bader Ginsburg made it 7–2.

Ginsburg was actually born Joan, but soon became known as 'Kiki' because she was a 'kicky baby'. Then she started school, where there were several other girls called Joan, so her mother added 'Ruth' to make things easier for the teacher. In 1956 she enrolled at Harvard Law School, one of nine women in a class of 500. The Dean asked them: 'How do you justify taking a spot from a qualified man?' Her husband Martin was also a student at Harvard, and when he was diagnosed with cancer Ruth attended classes and took notes for both of them. She typed up the papers Martin dictated to her. And served as editor of the *Harvard Law Review*. And looked after her young daughter.

In 1972 Ginsburg co-founded the Women's Rights Project

at the American Civil Liberties Union. She appeared before the Supreme Court in six gender-discrimination cases, winning five of them. The word 'gender' was deliberately chosen after Ginsburg's secretary suggested the word 'sex' might distract the male judges.

Bill Clinton appointed Ginsburg to the Supreme Court on 14 June 1993. When Clinton's Vice President, Al Gore, was sworn in for his second period of office in 1997, he specifically requested that Ginsburg administer his oath. In 2013 she became the first Supreme Court Justice to officiate at a same-sex wedding. She wears a different jabot (an item of lace neckwear) depending on which type of verdict she's delivering: if it's a majority opinion she chooses a yellow and cream one, while for dissenting opinions she wears black and gold. When researchers at the Cleveland Museum of Natural History named a new species of praying mantis in 2016, they opted for *Ilomantis ginsburgae*, as the insect's neckplate looks like a jabot. But they stated that the title also paid tribute to Ginsburg's gender-equality work: the species was the first praying mantis to be identified by the genitalia of its female.

Bobby Leach: second person to ride over Niagara Falls in a barrel

'If it was with my dying breath,' said Annie Taylor, the first person to ride over Niagara Falls in a barrel, 'I would caution anyone against attempting the feat.' The American had undertaken the stunt on 24 October 1901, her 63rd birthday, having tested her custom-made barrel two days previously by sending it over the Falls with a cat inside. The mattress fitted inside it allowed the animal to survive with nothing worse than a cut to the head. Taylor herself received the same injury in her own fall, but again, nothing worse. However, her aim – to make money by talking about the experience – didn't succeed. She earned very little, and most of that had to be spent on private detectives to track down the barrel when her manager ran off with it.

Ignoring her advice, British-born Bobby Leach repeated the Falls fall ten years later. A performer with the Barnum and Bailey circus, he boasted that anything Taylor could do, he could do better. Initially this didn't seem to be the case: he suffered much worse injuries than she had, including two broken kneecaps and a fractured jaw. But in the longer term he did outperform her: he enjoyed several years earning a living by giving lectures on his feat in the US, Canada and Britain, exhibiting his barrel and posing for pictures.

However, in 1926, on a publicity tour in New Zealand, Leach slipped on an orange peel and broke his leg. Infection set in, gangrene meant the leg had to be amputated, and further complications ensured that Bobby was dead within two months.

Jürg Marmet and Ernst Schmied: second team to conquer Mount Everest

The Swiss team that conquered the world's highest mountain in 1956 were delayed by a British newspaper, a fictional creature and some Indian bureaucrats – but they got there in the end.

Only four months after Edmund Hillary and Tenzing Norgay's triumph of May 1953, the Swiss Foundation for Alpine Research was given permission by the Nepalese government to undertake its own research in the Everest massif. The plan was to visit the following year, but soon afterwards it was announced that the *Daily Mail* were going to explore the same area in search of the Yeti. The Foundation therefore decided to postpone their trip.

It would be 1956 before the 10-man team finally sailed to Bombay (now Mumbai), where customs officials held them up for a week. But eventually they reached the Himalayas. It took 350 porters to load their 10 tons of equipment onto 22 ox carts. Some of it had been tested in a butcher's cold-storage room. There were explosives to blow up ice blocks, and wooden beams and ladders for crossing crevasses. The load would have been even heavier had Jürg Marmet, the team's oxygen expert, not designed new tanks, which at just six kilos were less than half the weight of those used by Hillary and Tenzing. Vital equipment, of course: at the top of Everest the air contains only a quarter of the oxygen found at sea level.

On 18 May two of the team, Ernst Reiss and Fritz Luchsinger, became the first people ever to climb Lhotse, the world's fourth-highest mountain. Its jagged peak means there is nowhere to sit, so the pair had to be particularly careful when taking their photographs.

On 22 May, the night before Marmet and his colleague Ernst Schmied made their attempt on Everest's peak, heavy snow fell on their tent, weighing it down so much that they had to clear it away to avoid being suffocated. Finally, at 2 p.m. on 23 May, they made their way to the summit.

Schmied attached the flags of Switzerland, Bern and Nepal to his ice pick so that Marmet could take photos. Unlike on the previous expedition, each man had his photo taken by the other. Hillary had taken Tenzing's picture, but when Tenzing offered to reciprocate, Hillary declined. Similarly – although in this case it was by mistake rather than on purpose – Neil Armstrong held the camera for all of his and Buzz Aldrin's time on the Moon: the only image of Armstrong is one of him reflected in Aldrin's visor.

The winds atop Everest were light, meaning that Marmet and Schmied could take off their oxygen masks and enjoy the views for nearly an hour. Then fog descended, forcing them to make a quick descent. The next day Dölf Reist and Hans Ruedi von Gunten followed them, becoming the first people ever to see previous climbers' footprints on the top of Everest. After that the expedition leader, Albert Eggler, decided that an approaching monsoon made it too risky for anyone else to attempt the summit, so the team descended.

Back home in Switzerland, the shoe firm Bally took out full-page adverts for their new reindeer-fur boots. The range was named 'On Top of the World'.

Min Bahadur Sherchan: second-oldest person to climb Mount Everest

Here we reach a tale that demonstrates the dangers of not being happy with second place. Min Bahadur Sherchan was born in 1931 in the tiny Nepalese village of Bhurung Tatopani. For a while he served in the Gurkha regiment of the British Army, at one point living in the UK. His thoughts first turned to mountaineering records in 1960, when as a Nepalese government liaison official he accompanied a Swiss expedition to Dhaulagiri, the seventh-highest peak in the world. At that point it had never been climbed, and Sherchan hoped that this expedition would also fail, leaving him free to go back and become the first person ever to conquer the mountain. Sadly the team succeeded – and Sherchan himself didn't even get to reach the top. 'I then lost all hope of setting a mountaineering record,' he said.

But in 2002, he realised that the title of 'oldest person ever to climb Everest' belonged to two 70-year-old Japanese men. At that point Nepalese sherpers held several records: youngest and fastest to climb the mountain, as well as most climbs and longest time at the top. 'I thought the [oldest person] record too should belong to a Nepali,' said Sherchan. He started training by going on long walks across his home country, on one occasion covering 640 miles in 20 days. Doctors warned of problems if he went above 3,000 metres, which only 'made me even more determined'. Finance was a problem: the Nepalese government refused to help, but some South Korean people raised the $50,000 needed. Getting insurance was another difficulty. But finally, on 25 May 2008, at the age of 76 years and 340 days, a great-grandfather five times over, Sherchan reached the top of Everest. 'At that moment I felt taller than the mountain.'

The following year's edition of *Guinness World Records*, however, gave the record to the Japanese climber Yuichiro Miura, who had conquered Everest aged a sprightly 75. Sherchan travelled to London to speak to Guinness about the error, then back home in Nepal he gathered together the documents, photos and eyewitness confirmations needed to authenticate his climb. Once these had been sent to Guinness, the 2010 edition listed him as the rightful holder of the title.

Yuichiro Miura, however, was clearly as determined to have the title as Sherchan had been. Despite having had two heart operations since his previous climb, on 23 May 2013, at the age of 80, he again reached the summit. So exhausted was he that he couldn't manage the climb back down, and had to be airlifted off the mountain.

Sherchan's reponse was as predictable as it was fateful: 'I want to take back my crown for Nepal and for the Brigade of Gurkhas.' Once again he began to train, 'with a weighted bag on my back . . . I must get to the top once more. I will not die happy unless I do.'

On 26 May 2017, at Everest base camp, preparing for his attempt, Min Bahadur Sherchan died of a suspected heart attack.

Robert Falcon Scott: second man to reach the South Pole

Scott's second place is one of the best-known in history. But a detail that often gets overlooked is one of the objects he found on his arrival at the South Pole. Discovering that the Norwegian Roald Amundsen had beaten him by five weeks, Scott recorded in his diary that 'the worst has happened . . . All the day dreams must go . . . Great God! This is an awful place and terrible enough for us to have laboured to it without the reward of priority.' He and his team discovered Amundsen's tent and some of his supplies. There was also a note confirming that the Norwegians had arrived there on 16 December 1911 ... and a letter from Amundsen to King Haakon VII of Norway, informing the monarch of his achievement. A covering note asked – very politely – that Scott should deliver the letter, in case Amundsen perished on the return journey. So as well as coming second, Scott would have had to be the person who *announced* that he had come second.

In the event, of course, it was Scott himself who failed to make it back to safety. The letter to King Haakon was found with his body. Though had he survived, he would have learned that – as so often – victory hadn't tasted quite as sweet as you might imagine. Amundsen later wrote: 'Never has a man achieved a goal so diametrically opposed to his wishes. The area around the North Pole – devil take it – had fascinated me since childhood, and now here I was at the South Pole. Could anything be more crazy?'

FAMILY

———◆———

Till someone else do us part: second spouses

Promising to love, honour and obey someone for as long as you both shall live is all very well, but things don't always work out that way. This doesn't mean, however, that people don't go back for a second (or third, or fourth . . .) time – the original 'triumph of hope over experience'. Another famous opinion about second marriages is that 'When a man marries his mistress, he creates a vacancy.' This quote is often credited to the financier Sir James Goldsmith, though he took it from the French actor Sacha Guitry, who had racked up five marriages. Not that the advice stopped Goldsmith from marrying his own mistress, Annabel Birley (he was already on his second marriage, his first wife having died). He subsequently left Birley for yet another mistress, though stopped short of marrying her.

Sometimes second marriages are caused by the need for an heir. In 1810 Napoleon said, 'Not tonight, Josephine, or indeed any other night in the future,' and divorced the woman who had been unable to provide him with a child. Some of his mistresses had borne his children, but an 'official' descendant was needed. Josephine hadn't always been in-fertile – she'd had two children by her first husband, one of whom, her daughter Hortense, had married Napoleon's brother. Her first husband had been executed during the French Revolution. Josephine herself had been imprisoned, and it's thought that the stress of this could have caused the later difficulties in conceiving. She hadn't always been Josephine either: until she met Napoleon she'd gone by her middle name, Rose, but the great leader didn't like that so she had to change it.

Napoleon's second wife was Marie Louise, the daughter of Archduke Francis of Austria, ruler of the Holy Roman Empire (which, as Voltaire pointed out, was neither holy, Roman nor an empire). The marriage was seen as a way of cementing relations between France and Austria, though as Marie Louise's great-aunt had been executed in France and Napoleon himself had fought several campaigns against her country, his intended wasn't entirely happy about the arrangement. 'Just to see the man would be the worst form of torture,' she said. And indeed at the wedding she didn't see him – it took place by proxy, her new husband being represented at the ceremony in Vienna by her own uncle. But when she travelled to France and actually met Napoleon, Marie Louise began to thaw. She told him: 'You are much better looking than your portrait.' Soon she was writing to her father: 'There is something very fetching and eager about him that is impossible to resist.' Napoleon, who initially remarked to an aide that he had 'married a womb', also warmed to the relationship. The following year the couple had a son. When Napoleon was forced to abdicate in 1814 he named his three-year-old offspring as successor, but no one accepted this and Napoleon II's 'reign' only lasted a few days.

Napoleon himself was forced into exile on the island of Elba. His wife did not accompany him. He had never stopped loving Josephine, and when she died shortly afterwards he locked himself in his room for two days. Her name was his final word when he died in 1821. His son survived him by only 11 years, dying of tuberculosis at the age of 21. Marie Louise married twice more, bearing three more children, and died in 1847.

Another ruler who switched spouses to try for an heir was Henry VIII. After his first wife, Catherine of Aragon, failed to produce a surviving son, he divorced her and married Anne Boleyn. He knew the family well, having already had an affair with her sister Mary. (Similarly, Prince Charles only met Diana because he was seeing her sister Sarah, though there's no suggestion – as there is with Henry VIII – that he added his wife's mother to his list of conquests.) Anne soon produced a daughter – who would grow up to be Elizabeth I – but after that she had two miscarriages. The fact that the second baby would have been a boy convinced Henry that the marriage was cursed, and he turned his attentions to Anne's lady-in-waiting, Jane Seymour (who in the 20th century would provide a stage name for the actress born Joyce Penelope Wilhelmina Frankenberg). The King had his wife arrested for adultery (with five men, one of whom was her own brother – if you're going to trump up a charge, trump it up in style), and she was executed on 19 May 1536. As a sign of respect Henry had the sentence commuted from burning to beheading. This was carried out by an expert swordsman brought over specially from France, rather than subject Anne to the common old axe. She knelt upright, in the French fashion, and her death took just a single stroke of the sword. Her memory lived on not just as the second element of the *aide mémoire* 'divorced, beheaded, died . . .', but also in the name of West Ham United's ground before they moved to the London Stadium in 2016. Commonly referred to as Upton Park, it was also known as the Boleyn Ground because the queen was believed to have stayed in a house on the site.

There are often similarities between someone's second spouse and their first. Margaret Thatcher was Denis's second wife, his first also having been called Margaret. With Charlie Chaplin the parallels went further: his first two wives were both 16-year-old actresses who were thought to be pregnant. As it turned out Mildred Harris wasn't, but Chaplin clearly had reason to believe she might have been, because he married her quickly to avoid a scandal. They soon divorced, but then the same thing happened again. This time the girl (Lita Grey) *was* pregnant, and in May 1925, less than six months after a hushed-up marriage in Mexico, she gave birth to Chaplin's first child, Charles Jnr. But again the relationship was unhappy. Lita filed for divorce, accusing Chaplin of having affairs and harbouring 'perverted sexual desires'. Copies of the document were sold to the public, and to minimise the bad publicity the 38-year-old star agreed to a payment of $600,000 (worth over $8m today) – at the time the largest-ever divorce settlement in the US. The money clearly didn't last: by the 1970s Grey was working as a clerk in a Beverly Hills department store.

For some people, however, the second set of wedding bells ring the changes. Arthur Miller met his first wife, Mary Grace Slattery, when they were university students together in Michigan. In 1956, he left her for Marilyn Monroe. Their marriage prompted the *Variety* magazine headline: 'Egghead Weds Hourglass'. Monroe converted to Judaism for the wedding ceremony, which led to all her films being banned in Egypt. But she didn't care. 'I hate Hollywood,' she told her new husband (her third). 'I don't want it any more. I want to live quietly in the country and just be there when you need me.' And to a friend she confided: 'I can identify with the Jews. Everybody's always out to get them, no matter what they do, like me.'

Initially the marriage worked well. Away from the film-industry spotlight Monroe enjoyed cooking, housework and taking care of Miller's two children (aged twelve and nine). The children adored her in return, and she also developed a good relationship with Miller's parents. But by 1960, as Monroe worked on what would be her last completed film, *The Misfits*, the relationship had deteriorated. Miller himself had written the screenplay to provide his wife with a serious role, but she objected to him basing parts of the character on her own life. By this time Monroe's drug addiction was so advanced that she would remain unconscious even as her make-up was applied. The couple divorced after filming was completed. Monroe died two years later.

The event in which Jacqueline Kennedy lost her first husband was one of the most famous of the 20th century. And when, five years later, JFK's brother Robert was also assassinated, Jackie began to fear. 'If they're killing Kennedys,' she said, 'then my children are targets ... I want to get out of this country.' That option was available via her long-standing friend Aristotle Onassis. The Greek shipping magnate had his own private island, Skorpios, and it was here, four months after Robert Kennedy's death, that Onassis and Jackie were married. This lost Jackie the Secret Service protection given to her as the widow of a US President. There were also rumours – due to the fact that Onassis was divorced and his first wife, Athina Livanos, was still alive – that 'Jackie O', as she was now known, might be excommunicated by the Catholic Church. The Church soon replied that this was 'nonsense'.

The couple achieved much of their privacy aboard the *Christina O*, the 325-foot yacht that Onassis had named after his daughter, and which in its previous guise as a naval frigate had taken part in the Normandy landings during World War II. The stools in the yacht's bar were upholstered with leather made from the foreskins of minke whales. 'Madame,' Onassis would say to female passengers, 'you are sitting on the largest penis in the world.' But the charming witticisms came to an end in 1975 when the tycoon died. Greek law limited the amount a non-Greek spouse could inherit, and after two years of legal argument Jackie had to settle for just $26m. Oh, and $150,000 a year for life. Gore Vidal was once asked how the world would have been different if in 1963 it had been the Soviet leader, Nikita Khrushchev, who'd been shot rather than President Kennedy. The main difference, he replied, was that 'Onassis probably wouldn't have married Mrs Khrushchev'.

Childish behaviour: second siblings

'First is the worst, second is the best, third is the one with the hairy chest.' Ignoring the questionable biology at the end of this famous statement, how does its middle measure up? Do second children really perform better than their elder siblings? Not if you believe a 2017 report based on data from Denmark and Florida, which found that second-borns were more likely to get suspended from school and eventually go to prison. But of course you can get statistics to say whatever you want – let's turn to some specific examples.

Second-born Richard Nixon got to be President of the United States (let's gloss over the fact that some people wanted him to go to prison as well). Like all but one of his four brothers, Nixon was named after an English king, in his case Richard the Lionheart. Donald Trump also got to be President, as well as a very stable genius, and although he wasn't a second-born (he was fourth) his father Fred, who built the fortune on which Donald based his own, was a second child. He also had the middle name Christ.

Someone with a fortune even larger than that of Trump is Bill Gates. Sandwiched between two sisters, Gates shares his first name with both his father and grandfather, which is why he was known in the family as 'Trey' (William Gates III). He and some fellow school students were banned from the Computer Center Corporation because they'd exploited bugs in the programmes to obtain free time on the machines. When they returned they offered to find more bugs if the CCC gave them extra time. Gates's own second child (Rory, born in 1999) can now look up at the ceiling of his father's purpose-built mansion near Seattle and read a quote from *The Great Gatsby:* 'He had come a long way to this blue lawn and his dream must have seemed so close he could hardly fail to grasp it.'

Fans of *Keeping Up with the Kardashians* will know that

Kim is a second child (behind Kourtney and ahead of Khloé and Rob). The name obviously suits go-getters intent on world domination – someone else with just one elder sibling is Kim Jong-un. One elder sibling by the same mother, that is. The North Korean ruler also has two half-siblings. Or rather had: the elder of the two, Kim Jong-nam, was poisoned in 2017, and many people think Kim Jong-un knows more about the death than he's letting on. Kim Jong-nam had once been tipped as his father's successor, but fell out of favour in 2001 when he embarrassed the regime by trying to enter Japan on a false passport so he could visit Tokyo Disneyland.

Michael Jackson's second child was a daughter. He had called his son Michael, and would go on to name his other son Prince Michael (commonly referred to as 'Blanket'), so the inconvenient fact of this child being female wasn't going to stop the King of Pop – he called her 'Paris-Michael'. Jackson himself was an eighth child. His second-oldest sibling was known as Jackie, though had actually been christened Sigmund, which in a family as complicated as that seems only appropriate.

Heir supply: royals who were second in line

A very special set of younger siblings can be found hanging from the branches of the royal family tree. Not only do they have the usual 'issues' associated with looking up to an older brother or sister, they also know that were it not for an accident of birth, they would have inherited the British crown.

Whether or not they *wanted* to inherit that crown is a

different matter. When the young princesses Elizabeth and Margaret learned (aged ten and six) that their father was to become King George VI, the younger girl asked her sister: 'Does this mean you'll become queen one day?' Elizabeth replied: 'Yes, I suppose it does.' 'Poor you,' came the response. As Elizabeth had already produced Prince Charles (and indeed Princess Anne) by the time she ascended the throne, Margaret could rest safe in the knowledge that the job would never be hers. The style in which she lived her life showed that she was glad to be (relatively) out of the limelight. Her social set was much racier than her sister's, though that did prove to be a problem when the man she loved (Group Captain Peter Townsend) was deemed off-limits as husband material because he'd been married before. Margaret had to content herself with a life of parties. Many were extravagant, and some were risqué, such as the gathering at which the film critic Kenneth Tynan showed his guests a blue movie. This proved a bit much even for Margaret, but thankfully another guest, the comedian Peter Cook, diffused the tension by providing a commentary to the film as though it were a commercial for the Cadbury's Flake chocolate bar. Within minutes everybody – the princess included – was crying with laughter.

A few generations previously the second in line had been Prince Alfred, the younger brother of the man who would become Edward VII. He was Queen Victoria's fourth child, but only her second son, and when he was born (1844) the royal family was still well over a century away from treating males and females equally in the line of succession. (This wasn't achieved until the Perth Agreement came into effect in 2015.) After a childhood attempt to pronounce his name went wrong, Alfred was always known to his family as 'Affie'. At the age of 14 he joined the navy as a midshipman. A possible diversion from this career path emerged in 1867, when King Otto of Greece died and his subjects held a referendum as to who should succeed him. The Greeks, wanting to ally themselves with the dominant world power, Britain, voted for Prince Alfred. But neither he nor his mother were interested in the idea, and Alfred continued with his life on the waves.

Also in 1867 he became the first member of the royal family to visit Australia, staying for several months. He enjoyed his time there, despite the fact that while he was in Sydney a gunman tried to assassinate him. A bullet entered Alfred's back, but someone wrestled the weapon from the assailant's hand, and received a gold watch for his efforts. Alfred had more luck in Ceylon (now Sri Lanka) in 1869, where the country's richest man, Charles Henry de Soysa, hosted a dinner at which the prince ate off gold plates with gold cutlery inlaid with precious stones. As if that wasn't enough, de Soysa renamed his home Alfred House.

In 1874 Alfred married the Grand Duchess Maria Alexandrovna of Russia. It was in honour of this occasion that the Marie biscuit (still eaten today) was created. The prince played an important role in the founding of the Royal College of Music, and was indeed a violinist himself. But if we're to believe Sir Henry Ponsonby, Queen Victoria's Private Secretary, Alfred's enthusiasm exceeded his talent – having heard him perform at a dinner party, Ponsonby wrote: 'Fiddle out of tune and noise abominable.'

Alfred died in 1900, the third of Victoria's children to be outlived by her (she died six months later). Among the ways in which he's commemorated are several in South Africa, where he had proved popular on a visit. The harbour in Cape Town is known as the Victoria and Alfred Waterfront (the prince had tipped the first load of rocks into the sea to commence its construction). Port Elizabeth's stadium for the 2010 football World Cup was built in Prince Alfred Park, while the same city's chapter of the Memorable Order of Tin Hats (a military veterans' association) is known as the Prince Alfred Shellhole.

Another second son (but third child – poor old Princess Augusta, Duchess of Brunswick, was passed over) was Prince Edward, the Duke of York and Albany. His elder brother became George III, making Edward himself the heir presumptive to the throne. An heir presumptive is different from an heir apparent: the latter is someone who cannot be moved from their position of first in line, unlike an heir presumptive, whose primacy depends on nothing changing. In Edward's case what changed was George III having a child in 1762 (a son who would go on to become George IV).

George was a serious person, but Edward took the Princess Margaret route and had fun. He enjoyed practical jokes. Indeed his childhood pranks once got him into trouble with his mother, who banned him from her rooms and ordered her staff not to admit him. Entering the music room with her guests after dinner, she found Edward, and immediately asked which servant had let him in. 'Don't be angry, my dear mother,' said the young prince, 'nobody has disobeyed you. I came in through the middle window, by the help of the lamplighter's ladder.' His smile melted his mother's heart, and he was forgiven.

As an adult Edward socialised with some rather

questionable characters, and enjoyed the company of many different women. In 1767, aged 28, he attended a party in Toulon in France, where he was taken ill. Ignoring advice to rest, he carried on towards Genoa, where he was due to meet a mistress. On the way he stopped in Monaco, whose ruler, Honoré III, rushed home to welcome his distinguished visitor. This entailed assembling the Monegasque guard so they could salute Edward and fire their artillery in his honour. While this happened Edward had to stand in full uniform in hot weather, which only worsened his condition. He retreated to Honoré's palace, but nothing could be done to save him: he died on 17 September. Honoré organised a full lying-in-state and a magnificent send-off for the body. By way of thanks George III sent him two of Edward's finest racehorses. The room in which Edward died is still known as the York Room. Also named after the prince were Cape York, the northenmost point of Australia, and Prince Edward Augustus, George III's fourth son, who was born the day after Edward was buried at Westminster Abbey.

TV AND FILM

◆

David Edwards: second person to win £1m on *Who Wants to Be a Millionaire?*

When 53-year-old physics teacher David Edwards reached £250,000 on *Who Wants to Be a Millionaire?*, he commented that it was 'probably more than I've been paid throughout my working life'. So every step from then on – when he could lose almost all of the money – was a risk. As indeed it had been for the first winner, Judith Keppel, who had money troubles at the time, despite being descended from the subject of her million-pound question, Henry II.

Edwards clearly knew his stuff: a *Mastermind* champion in 1990, he also reached the final of Channel 4's *Fifteen to One* and was a member of the Welsh national quiz team. And he was thorough: after calculating how many premium-rate phone calls he would need to make to get selected for *Who Wants to Be a Millionaire?*, he put aside £1,000 to pay for them. He rehearsed his 'Fastest Finger' technique. This paid off when, at his recording on 10 April 2001, he put four words – 'fathom', 'folly', 'first' and 'fence' – into alphabetical order quicker than anyone else. (Depressingly, only four out of the ten contestants managed the task at all.) Indeed, you could say his preparation had started at the age of seven, when his mother bought him a ninepenny book of facts in Woolworths: 'I went through it and memorised all the capital cities, everything.'

He was rarely in much doubt on his run to the top prize. He knew who, according to legend, was poisoned by the composer Salieri (Mozart), what kind of creature a grackle is (bird) and which type of people were members of the 19th-century Newlyn School (painters). The only time he struggled was on the £125,000 question: 'What is the real first name of Home Secretary Jack Straw?' The options were Justin, James, John and Joseph. Using his 'Ask the Audience' lifeline produced a 62 per cent verdict for John. Then he phoned a friend, or rather his son, Richard, who he said was often 'comatose'. Presenter Chris Tarrant asked if they should tell Richard how much was at stake. 'Yes,' replied David. 'Concentrate the mind.' But Richard didn't have a clue. 'Never mind,' said his father. 'Back to sleep.' The last lifeline, 50/50, left just James and John. At first Edwards thought he'd take the 'less likely' option, but eventually gambled on John. It was correct.

By the time he reached the million-pound question, Edwards said that 'In a masochistic sort of way I'm enjoying it.' He was enjoying it even more a couple of minutes later, after knowing that the seeds of *Quercus robur* would grow not into flowers, vegetables or grain but into trees. After the recording he and his wife Viv were 'whisked back to a hotel, of the sort which is so posh, they don't provide you with a kettle'. Before the evening was out a *Sun* reporter had found his home in Staffordshire, and over the next fortnight (before the programme was transmitted) his village was besieged by the press. 'I'm pleased to say,' said Viv, 'that the pub, the garage and the shop did very well out of them.' For a while David carried on teaching. 'The kids now say "Give us a tenner, sir."'

Edwards would be one of only four millionaires created by the show. (It could have been five, had Major Charles Ingram not cheated his way to the money.) In America the second winner was Dan Blonsky, one of whose questions revealed that when she used her CB radio in the White House, Gerald Ford's wife Betty went by the handle 'First Mama'. The first US winner, John Carpenter, had phoned his father on the final question. He said: 'Hi Dad. I don't really need your help. I just wanted to let you know I'm going to win the million dollars.'

The British father–son relationship ended up playing more of a role in the show. Not only was Richard Edwards asked for help by his father, he himself later appeared as a contestant on the programme and won £125,000. Appropriate for someone his father had always referred to as 'Rich'.

The Body Show: second programme on Channel 4

'Safe exercises for people at home' doesn't sound like the most gripping television. The instruction 'Imagine you are like a fountain' is slightly more intriguing – but it wasn't enough to keep *The Body Show* on air for very long.

The signs were there from the beginning. The new channel's opening offer, *Countdown*, attracted 3.7 million viewers at 4.45 p.m. on Tuesday 2 November 1982. But only 2.1 million stayed on (or tuned in) for *The Body Show* at 5.30 p.m.

This saw leotard-clad dancer Yvonne Ocampo demonstrating keep-fit exercises which anyone could tackle, no matter their age or ability (some were even achievable by people in wheelchairs). Ocampo was 34. In the 1960s she had danced as a member of the famous Bluebell Girls at Le Lido in Paris, and in 1975 was cast as 'Moroccan maiden' in the John Huston film *The Man Who Would Be King*. She appeared in the *Benny Hill Show*, and during her time at London's Raymond Revuebar had appeared in a documentary film titled *And They Call Me Pussy Dynamite*. Her other work included handling a dog for one of Ringo Starr's pop videos.

Countdown is still a fixture in the Channel 4 listings over thirty years later. *The Body Show* lasted only a few episodes. According to one history of independent TV in Britain: 'It drew protests from viewers in the North of England and Scotland that they couldn't take part in the exercises so soon after their high tea, and in the South most people were not back from work in time to take part.'

1930: second Academy Awards ceremony

Things normally get more complicated the longer they go on. The second Academy Awards ceremony is a rare example of a second being simpler than its first. At least in the number of categories: the inaugural ceremony, held on 16 May 1929 at the Hollywood Roosevelt Hotel, had 12 categories – the one held at Los Angeles' Ambassador Hotel on 3 April 1930 trimmed this to seven.

That said, the event was longer. The previous year's had lasted just 15 minutes. (The Roosevelt would go on to host several 'Razzies', the Golden Raspberry Awards that commemorate the worst films of the year.) The 1930 ceremony was a less rushed affair, taking place in the Ambassador's Cocoanut Grove nightclub, where a few years previously an unknown Joan Crawford had won dance competitions with her Charleston and her Black Bottom. In 1968 the hotel would also be the scene of Robert Kennedy's assassination.

The ceremony (hosted by William C. DeMille, Cecil B.'s brother) remains the only one at which no film won more than one award. Best Actor, for his portrayal of the Cisco Kid in *In Old Arizona*, was Warner Baxter. (The film's director, Raoul Walsh, had been due to star in the film too, but on location a jackrabbit jumped through the window of a car he was driving, causing him to lose an eye and ending his acting career.) As a teenager Baxter had been made homeless by the 1906 San Francisco earthquake, he and his mother having to live in Golden Gate Park for eight days. As well as acting he pursued a career as an inventor: he co-created a searchlight that attached to revolvers and let you aim more clearly at night, and also made a radio device that let the drivers of emergency vehicles change traffic lights as they approached them, so speeding their progress through intersections.

Best Actress was Mary Pickford for her role in *Coquette*. One of the biggest stars of her day, she was among the first to be credited by name (film performers before then had usually received no billing). In 1909 she appeared in no fewer than 51 movies. She was one of the 36 founding members of the Academy of Motion Picture Arts and Sciences, and her husband Douglas Fairbanks was its first president.

Best Director was Frank Lloyd – he is still the only winner

whose film (in this case *The Divine Lady*) wasn't nominated for Best Picture. Best Cinematography, for *White Shadows in the South Seas*, went to Clyde De Vinna, an amateur radio enthusiast who took a portable transmitter with him on every location shoot. Three years later, filming *Eskimo* in Alaska, he kept the crew in touch with their base. But because the shack in which he worked had been made airtight to keep out the cold, he was overcome by carbon monoxide fumes from his oil heater. Fortunately, at the time he was in contact with an amateur radio enthusiast in New Zealand, who knew from De Vinna's faltering keystrokes that he must be in trouble. This operator transmitted a call for help to Hawaii, from where someone in turn relayed a message to Alaska, and De Vinna was reached in time to be saved.

Best Art Direction and Interior Decoration went to Cedric Gibbons for *The Bridge of San Luis Rey*. Gibbons would end up being nominated for Oscars 38 times, winning 11 of them, but his link with the award is even stronger than that: he designed it. His statuette has remained virtually unchanged since he created it in 1928 (the only tweak being a minor streamlining of the base). Modelled on the Mexican actor Emilio Fernandez (who took some persuading to pose nude), Oscar is 13.5 inches tall, weighs 8.5 pounds, and stands on a reel of film whose five spokes represent the original branches of the Academy (actors, writers, directors, producers and technicians). The early awards were made of gold-plated bronze, but within a few years this gave way to gold-plated Britannia metal, an alloy similar to pewter prized for its silver colour and smoothness. (Though not favoured by George Orwell, who complained in his essay 'A Nice Cup of Tea' that Britannia teapots produced an inferior cuppa to chinaware ones.) During the World War II metal shortage, Oscars were made from plaster, the Academy replacing them with proper ones after the war was over. In 2016 the Academy reverted to bronze. There are competing theories as to why Oscar is Oscar: the Academy's first secretary claimed he looked like a cousin of hers with that name, while Bette Davis (a president of the Academy) is said to have named him after her first husband, band leader Harmon Oscar Nelson. Either way, Oscar Hammerstein II is still the only Oscar to win an Oscar.

The second Awards ceremony (the informal 'Oscars' nickname wasn't officially adopted by the Academy until 1939) kept the winners' names secret until the evening itself – unlike the previous year, when they'd been announced three months in advance. The names were still given to the *Los Angeles Times* ready for publication at 11 p.m. This arrangement continued until 1941, when the newspaper announced the winners too early, as a result of which the sealed envelope was introduced. The accountancy firm PricewaterhouseCoopers have been in charge of the secrecy ever since (and retained their contract even after the 2017 error that led to *La La Land* rather than *Moonlight* being announced as the winner). Until 2010 Oscars were presented with blank nameplates, the winner returning it to the Academy for several weeks while it was engraved. In 2010 nameplates were engraved for every nominee, the unused majority being recycled. But since then winners have been able to get their names engraved onto their statuette at the post-ceremony party.

Tenderloin: second talking movie

In 1928, the year after Al Jolson's *The Jazz Singer* had become the first 'talkie', Warner Bros followed up with another film utilising their 'Vitaphone' system. This didn't actually print the soundtrack onto the film itself, but played it separately on phonograph records, the turntable linked to the projector's motor. The name came from the Latin word for 'life' and the Greek word for 'sound', just as 'television' comes from the Greek for 'far' and the Latin for 'see'.

The plot of *Tenderloin* concerns Rose Shannon, a nightclub dancer in the Tenderloin district of New York, who loves Chuck White, a member of a criminal gang that uses the club as its hangout. Rose was played by Dolores Costello, the 'Goddess of the Silent Screen', whose lisp proved a threat to her career now that films were going to have sound. Two years' voice coaching, however, finally made her comfortable about her words being heard on screen. What couldn't be fixed was the damage wrought on Shannon's complexion by the make-up used in movies at the time. Gradually her career petered out, and she spent the final part of her life in seclusion, managing an avocado farm. Her granddaughter is the actress Drew Barrymore.

Chuck was played by Conrad Nagel, who would go on to make three appearances as host of the Academy Awards. The gap between two of these (1932 and 1953) is the longest of any Oscars host. Another member of the cast was Mitchell Lewis, who later had an uncredited appearance in *The Wizard of Oz* as the captain of the Winkie Guards.

The movie's director was Michael Curtiz, born Mihály Kertész in Hungary and a competitor for his country's fencing team at the 1912 Olympics in Stockholm. His directing work in Europe had included the 1922 Austrian classic *Sodom und Gomorrha*. After his move to America, Warner Bros tried him out on smaller films to see whether he was up to their high standards. The first of these was another crime story, *The Third Degree*. Curtiz spoke barely any English and knew nothing about American gangsters, so convinced a sheriff to let him spend a week in a Los Angeles jail. 'When I came out I knew what I needed for the picture,' he said. His work ethic often went unmatched by his actors, of whom he tended to have a low opinion. Acting, he said, 'is fifty per cent a big bag of tricks. The other fifty per cent should be talent and ability, although it seldom is.'

Curtiz went on to have a successful career, but his problems with English never entirely disappeared. Directing *Casablanca*, he told the props master that for one scene he wanted a poodle. Confused and irritated that Curtiz hadn't mentioned this before, the props master nevertheless tracked down a poodle and took it to the director. 'Vat I vant with this goddam dog?!' shouted Curtiz. The props master reminded him of the instruction. 'I vant a *poodle*!' came the reply. 'A poodle of water in the street!'

One of Curtiz's malapropisms ended up as the title for David Niven's second volume of memoirs. During the filming of *The Charge of the Light Brigade*, when the action called for riderless horses to appear, Curtiz shouted: 'Bring on the empty horses!' Niven and his co-star Errol Flynn dissolved into laughter at this, prompting Curtiz to round on them: 'You people!' he yelled. 'You think I know fuck nothing! Well, let me tell you, I know fuck all!'

Like *The Jazz Singer*, *Tenderloin* wasn't a full talkie – there were still sections without sound. The fact that the movie contained spoken dialogue might have astounded audiences raised on silent films, but this wasn't enough to stop them laughing at the abysmal quality of the lines themselves. 'Mitchell Lewis is capable as the "Professor",' wrote the *New York Times* critic Mordaunt Hall, 'but words such as he has to utter would destroy the value of any acting ... (T)he spectators were moved to loud mirth during the spoken episodes of this lurid film.' There were four talking sequences in the film. After open laughter (for all the wrong reasons) during the premiere, Warner Bros cut two of them.

Patrick Troughton: second actor to play Doctor Who

This second brought a very particular sort of pressure: the knowledge that no one had expected there to *be* a second, and the awareness that if it went wrong there wouldn't be a third.

Doctor Who first hit Britain's television screens on Saturday 23 November 1963. This was the day after the assassination of John F. Kennedy, and with the world still in shock the programme made little impact. So the BBC repeated the first episode the following week, immediately before the second episode, and gradually the series gained a following. William Hartnell played the title role, but by 1966 it was obvious his days were numbered. 'Bill had become very difficult to work with,' says Anneke Wills, who portrayed the Doctor's sidekick Polly. 'We had to be very generous and kind and pick up his lines.' This could have meant the end of the show – but then the idea formed of getting another actor to carry on the role. Several auditioned, such as Michael Hordern, who would go on to voice *Paddington Bear*. But Hartnell himself said: 'There's only one man in England who can take over, and that's Patrick Troughton.'

Troughton was an established TV character actor: in 1953 he played the first Robin Hood on the small screen. (Half a century later his grandson Sam Troughton would play one of Robin's colleagues in another BBC adaptation. Another grandson is Harry Melling, who played Dudley Dursley in the *Harry Potter* films, while yet another is Jim Troughton, who played cricket for England.) Patrick had also played Winston Smith in a BBC Radio version of *Nineteen Eighty-Four*, and taken a minor role in the Joseph L. Mankiewicz film *Escape*, one of whose stars was William Hartnell.

Troughton first toyed with playing the Doctor as a 'tough sea captain', or as a piratical figure in a turban with his face blacked up. But eventually he adopted the idea of the programme's creator Sydney Newman, and made the Doctor a 'cosmic hobo', much scruffier than Hartnell's portrayal. He wore an oversized black frock coat, baggy orange and black trousers and a bow tie. His hair was deliberately messy. Unusual garb was nothing new to him: as a member of the Royal Naval Volunteer Reserve during World War II Troughton had kept warm on the North Sea by wearing a tea cosy on his head.

At first it wasn't entirely clear that Troughton was the same character – in the first episode he referred to Hartnell's Doctor in the third person. But when a Dalek recognised him it became clear that Troughton was indeed the Doctor, and the transformation was accepted by viewers. 'It was entirely up to Patrick that the audience did [accept him],' said Anneke Wills, who continued in the role of Polly. 'You couldn't resist him.' The appeal was helped by Troughton's reluctance to give interviews. 'I think acting is magic,' he said. 'If I tell you all about myself it will spoil it.' The same secrecy applied in his private life. Despite having left his wife for another woman shortly after the birth of their third child, Troughton maintained a front of still living with the family. He did it so convincingly that his own mother died without discovering the truth. The experience didn't put Troughton's son David off following his father into the profession. He once played Bolingbroke in *Richard II*, insisting that the audience stand up when he was crowned king. He even did this the night Prince Charles attended. Charles complied.

Like his predecessor, Troughton served three years as Doctor Who, quitting to avoid typecasting. He advised Peter Davison (the fifth Doctor) to do likewise, which the actor did. Davison (whose daughter Georgia grew up to marry David Tennant, the tenth Doctor) cites Troughton as his favourite Doctor, as do his successors Colin Baker, Sylvester McCoy and Matt Smith. In fact it was from Troughton that Smith took the idea for his bow tie.

Patrick Troughton died aged 67 of a heart attack in 1987, while attending a sci-fi convention in America, where he had taken part in discussions about *Doctor Who*. To the annoyance of Whovians everywhere, only two of his first fourteen episodes survived the BBC's practice of wiping archive tapes. But his legacy lives on. In 2017 a US news website ran an article about a second doctor being arrested in a malpractice case. The computer algorithm that chooses the site's pictures read the words 'Second Doctor' – and inserted a picture of Troughton.

Ali Osman: second character to speak in *EastEnders*

In typically cheery style, *EastEnders* started life with a death. A murder, to be precise: Den Watts, Ali Osman and Arthur Fowler broke down the door of Reg Cox, who (we would later discover) had been killed by Nick Cotton. Dirty Den's opening line has become the stuff of soap-opera folklore: 'Stinks in here, dunnit?' The next character to speak that February night in 1985? Ali Osman, with the single-word line, 'Reg?' Den replied: 'Well he ain't gonna answer now if he didn't answer before, is he?'

Osman was one of the 23 original characters created by the programme's writers Tony Holland and Julia Smith. Keen to reflect the racial mix of east London, they included a Turkish-Cypriot café owner, though originally called him Chris. When they realised this meant a Christian name for a Muslim character they changed it to Ali. They described him as 'basically lazy, and a gambler. Not (yet) a compulsive gambler – but he is a passionate one . . . He's a bit of a peacock. He expects to be waited on hand and foot.' This made for a stormy relationship with his British wife Sue: one critic described them as the 'Diet Coke version' of Den and Angie Watts, who ran Walford's pub the Queen Vic in similarly argumentative fashion.

Strange as it may seem given the subsequent rivalry between *EastEnders* and *Coronation Street*, Granada Television were happy to grant Julia Smith unrestricted access to the established programme's set for a month so she could pick up some tips. Some people at the BBC worried that viewers wouldn't watch a soap set in the South. But Smith thought that viewers in the North would accept it, just as viewers in the South accepted a soap set in the North, while viewers in the Midlands wouldn't mind where it was set as long as it wasn't the Midlands. Working titles included *Round the Houses*, *Round the Square*, *Square Dance* and *East 8*. The last one got the nod for a while, until casting agents repeatedly thought the programme was called *Estate*. Only then was the fictional postcode E20 created for Walford (it has since had to share it with London's Olympic Park). Smith hit on the title when she found herself asking the casting agents if they had any 'real East Enders on their books'. But she felt 'Eastenders' looked ugly when written down, so turned the second 'e' into a capital.

Ali Osman was played by Nejdet Salih, who, like the character, had been born in London of Turkish-Cypriot descent. He left the show in 1989 after 143 episodes. His subsequent work included the 1992 film *Carry on Columbus*, as well as the first two *Pirates of the Caribbean* movies. But despite changing his name to Nej Adamson, he found it hard to avoid that taint of Walford. 'I have had to live with Ali for 25 years,' he said in 2010. 'I'm just trying to get on with my life. I don't give interviews. I am still acting but it is hard when to everyone I'm still Ali from the café.'

A different path was followed by Adamson's one-time girlfriend Linda Davidson, who also starred in the early years of *EastEnders* as the troubled punk Mary Smith. After leaving the programme she eventually stopped acting, turning instead to writing for the internet. By the mid-1990s she was in charge of all the BBC's drama websites – including that of *EastEnders*.

George Lazenby: second actor to play James Bond

George Lazenby's inheritance of 007 duties was the complete opposite of Patrick Troughton's work as Doctor Who: despite some good reviews for his actual performance, the whole experience ended up as an unmitigated disaster.

Forget the pedantic point that the spy had already been portrayed on American television by Barry Nelson (who played him as 'Jimmy' Bond) and on South African radio by Bob Holness (later the host of the British TV quiz *Blockbusters*). We're talking here about the official Bond films – and by the time Sean Connery hung up his toupee in 1967, the franchise had become the hottest thing in cinema. Various people were approached to be Connery's successor, among them Peter Snow, still several years away from taking charge of the BBC's 'swingometer' on election nights. (At 6 feet 5 inches he was too tall: 'They said they'd have to put the girls on soapboxes.') Then one day, as producer Albert R. 'Cubby' Broccoli was having his hair cut, in the next chair he noticed a male model called George Lazenby. Originally from Australia, Lazenby had sold cars on Park Lane before being spotted by a talent scout. His advertising work – such as a campaign for Fry's Turkish Delight – earned him £25,000 a year. Broccoli asked him to audition for Bond. Lazenby went to Sean Connery's Savile Row tailors, who told him it would take six months to make a suit, 'but when I was on my way out of the door, they found one that he had left there'. Lazenby wore it to the audition, having had his hair cut by Connery's barber, and got the role. *On Her Majesty's Secret Service* would be his first-ever movie.

Even before it was released, however, Lazenby said he was done with 007. The producers had 'disregarded everything I suggested simply because I hadn't been in the film business like them for about a thousand years'. His co-star Diana Rigg sided with the producers, calling Lazenby 'utterly, un-believably . . . bloody impossible', and saying she could 'no longer cater for his obsession with himself'.

Lazenby admitted that others, including his parents, thought him 'insane' for giving up the role. But influenced by his agent saying that Bond would be seen as archaic in the 1970s (*On Her Majesty's Secret Service* came out in the last year of the 1960s), he enrolled to study drama at Durham University. He made a film in 1971 called *Universal Soldier*. It bombed. By 1973 he was 'flat broke', and arranged to meet Bruce Lee in Hong Kong to discuss starring in Lee's next film. However, on the day they were due to have lunch Lee died. By 1978 Lazenby was placing an advert in *Variety* asking for acting jobs, even telling a journalist he was prepared to work for nothing.

Eventually he did get other roles, though some of them were parodies harking back to his time as Bond. Typical was a 2012 Canadian TV comedy sketch called 'Help, I've Skyfallen and I Can't Get Up'. Lazenby's name is now a byword for brief appearances as a character. Paul McGann, for instance, calls himself 'the George Lazenby of Doctor Who', having starred as the Timelord for a short spell in 1996. At least Lazenby can comfort himself with the fact that he holds several 007 records: he was the youngest Bond ever (29), the only non-British Bond, and the only Bond ever to receive a Golden Globe for his portrayal of the spy.

Isaac Hayes: second African-American man to win an Oscar

At the 44th Academy Awards ceremony in 1972, Best Original Song was won by Isaac Hayes for his theme to *Shaft*, the film about (to quote the theme itself) 'the black private dick that's a sex machine to all the chicks'. Elsewhere in the lyrics Hayes is about to call John Shaft a 'bad mother****er', but the backing singers interrupt him. Nevertheless the line 'you're damn right!' makes this the first Billboard Hot 100 number one to include a swear word. Heaven knows what Angela Lansbury thought of all this. She was the performer of a rival for the award, one of the songs from *Bedknobs and Broomsticks*.

The first African-American man to win an Oscar had been Sidney Poitier in 1964, for his role in *Lilies of the Field*. The first African-American person to win an Oscar was Hattie McDaniel, who took Best Supporting Actress in 1940 for portraying the servant Mammy in *Gone with the Wind*. Despite its acclaim at the time, the film is often criticised these days for perpetuating black stereotypes. In 2017 its 34-year run of annual screenings at the Orpheum Theatre in Memphis came to an end.

Hayes's 1972 triumph must have been all the sweeter because he had originally auditioned for, and been denied, the title role of the film itself. The producers chose Richard Roundtree instead, but liked Hayes so much they offered him the chance to write the score. The resulting songs won him not only an Oscar but a Golden Globe and a Grammy as well. It was the first time the Best Original Song Oscar had gone to someone who'd both written and performed the song in question. Hayes thanked 'most of all' his grandmother (he'd been raised largely by his grandparents in Tennessee): 'In a few days it's her eightieth birthday, and this is her present from me.'

MUSIC

◆

'Massachusetts': second song played on Radio 1

The Bee Gees were actually in New York when they wrote 'Massachusetts' (the St Regis Hotel in Manhattan, to be precise). In fact at that point they had never been to Massachusetts. As Robin Gibb put it, the brothers just 'loved the word . . . there is always something magic about American place names. It only works with British names if you do it as a folk song. Roger Whittaker did that with "Durham Town".'

The song is a response to the San Francisco hippy scene, the lights having gone out in Massachusetts because everyone had left for the West Coast. The protagonist has followed them but is now homesick.

On 5 November 1967, a few weeks after it was played after The Move's 'Flowers in the Rain' which had launched Radio 1, the song became the Bee Gees' first UK number one. But for Robin Gibb that day brought mixed blessings: he was involved in the Hither Green rail crash, which killed 49 people. Gibb and his girlfriend Molly were uninjured, but Robin remembers 'sitting at the side of the carriage, watching the rain pour down, fireworks go off and the blue lights of the ambulance whirring. It was like something out of a Spielberg film.' The sight of people being carried on stretchers 'all got too much for me. I knew that I couldn't help anyone, and I couldn't cope with that . . . I had a delayed reaction – in the days that followed I started crying and crying and couldn't stop.'

'Massachusetts' might not have the place in trivia history that 'Flowers in the Rain' achieved – but at least it made the Bee Gees some serious money. The Move, however, fell foul of a publicity stunt by their manager Tony Secunda, who released a postcard showing (for some reason) the then Prime Minister Harold Wilson naked, and implying that he was having an affair with his secretary Marcia Williams. Wilson sued. He won, and the High Court ordered that all royalties from the song be donated to a charity of Wilson's choice. At the time most of the cash went to the Spastics Society and Stoke Mandeville Hospital. But the arrangement continues to this day, and by the 1990s Wilson's trust had extended the list of beneficiaries to include the Oxford Operatic Society and Bolton Lads Club.

'You Better Run' by Pat Benatar: second video played on MTV

By summer 1981 Pat Benatar already had form in the 'second' stakes. The album from which 'You Better Run' was taken – *Crimes of Passion* – was her second, and would end up selling over 5 million copies without reaching number one. Its top placing was number two: it had the misfortune to approach the chart's upper reaches just as John Lennon was shot dead in December 1980. His *Double Fantasy* album kept Benatar off the top spot for five weeks. Several months later, on 1 August, the revolutionary new television channel MTV chose 'You Better Run' as the second video they showed. The first had been 'Video Killed the Radio Star' by The Buggles. Both songs were intended as signals of intent to the radio industry.

Benatar had been inspired to start her musical career after attending a Liza Minnelli concert in Richmond, Virginia, where the 18-year-old was working as a bank teller. An early engagement was as a singing waitress in a nightclub called The Roaring Twenties, but eventually she secured a record deal. 'You Better Run' was the first single from *Crimes of Passion* – the second, 'Hit Me With Your Best Shot', would become one of Benatar's biggest hits. Its writer, Eddie Schwartz, came up with the title after taking part in a pillow-punching therapy session in Toronto.

Benatar's later work has veered away from her pop-rock beginnings. In 2011, she announced that she was 'working on a Christmas album and a novel about the second coming of Christ'.

Back in Black by AC/DC: second-bestselling album of all time

Thriller gets all the attention with its 65 million sales, but that's partly because of Michael Jackson's colourful (and eventually tragic) life. AC/DC are deliberately low-key ('we like to stay below the radar', as long-time lead singer Brian

Johnson put it), so the 50 million sales of *Back in Black* get relatively little attention.

The bell you hear at the beginning of the album, on the track 'Hell's Bells', was made specially for the band. They'd tried to record the Denison Bell in Loughborough's war-memorial tower, but the noise of pigeons flying close by meant that the mobile recording unit had to leave without the necessary 'clean' take. At the same time the band were having a replica of the bell made to take out on tour with them – it was touch and go whether it would be finished in time to make it onto the album, but eventually the manufacturers managed it. The replica was lighter than the original (a paltry one ton rather than four), but still presented AC/ DC's roadies with a challenge every night. Eventually, at a gig in Frankfurt, the chain snapped. The plummeting bell nearly crushed guitarist Angus Young, and a decision was taken that the time had finally come to retire it.

'Hell's Bells' played a key role after the 1993 US military raid to capture Mogadishu's Mohamed Farrah Aidid, which inspired the film *Black Hawk Down*. American helicopter pilot Michael Durant was being held by Somali militiamen somewhere in the city, but his colleagues didn't know where. Remembering that 'Hell's Bells' was his favourite song, they tied loudspeakers to a helicopter and flew it over the city, playing the track at full volume. 'I hear this "bong",' said Durant later, 'then I hear the beginning of "Hell's Bells" start up. It was an incredible moment.'

Although Durant's back had been broken when his helicopter crashed, he still managed to crawl to the window and wave a shirt through the bars. 'Immediately following the song I hear this voice saying: "Mike, we won't leave here without you.'" Nor did they. After his rescue, Durant eventually recovered from his injuries.

'You Belong to Me': second single to top the UK charts

The first chart of the bestselling singles in the UK appeared on 14 November 1952. It was topped – as it would be for the next eight weeks – by Al Martino's 'Here in my Heart'. But at number 12 was the single that would eventually dislodge Martino from his perch: 'You Belong to Me' by Jo Stafford.

Written by the American Chilton Price, whose previous work had included the song 'Slow Poke' (retitled 'Slow Coach' in the UK, probably wisely), 'You Belong to Me' is a ballad reminding the singer's true love that no matter what happens or where they go, their real home is with the singer. With such a beautiful sentiment it's entirely understandable that Bob Dylan's 1992 version features in the movie *Natural Born Killers*. Other versions have appeared in *Shrek*, *Down and Out in Beverly Hills* (sung by Bette Midler to Nick Nolte) and the TV show *Ally McBeal*.

Jo Stafford was born in 1917. In 1933, while rehearsing to play the lead in her school musical, she felt the stage begin to shake: it was an earthquake, which soon destroyed the entire building. At the age of 20 she and her two sisters got work writing the arrangements for the Fred Astaire movie *A Damsel in Distress*. Their version of 'Nice Work If You Can Get It' had to be altered because Astaire struggled with it. As Stafford said: 'The man with the syncopated shoes couldn't do the syncopated notes.'

During World War II Stafford's concerts for American

servicemen earned her the nickname 'GI Jo'. One veteran of the Pacific campaign told her that the Japanese used to play her record over loudspeakers, to try and induce feelings of homesickness in the Americans so that they'd surrender. After the war Stafford appeared on Voice of America radio programmes, the US government's overseas exercise in anti-Communist broadcasting. A magazine article of the time was headlined 'Jo Stafford: Her Songs Upset Joe Stalin'. In 1946, for NBC, she also took part in the first commercial radio broadcast from an airplane.

After Martino's marathon stint at the top of the British charts, 'You Belong to Me' only lasted a single week. But the following year Jo Stafford notched up another second – she followed Bing Crosby in selling 25 million records for the Columbia label. And her time with the troops during the war had given her a wide knowledge of military matters. Years later at a dinner party she got into an argument with a retired officer about the fighting off the Philippines island of Mindanao. 'Madam, I was there,' he said. But a few days later she received a letter of apology from him, saying he'd consulted the records and she was right.

'Volare': second single to top the US charts

America was a few years behind Britain in organising a 'hit parade': it was 1958 before the country had a unified chart (there were several different ones prior to that). The first single to top the Billboard Hot 100 was Ricky Nelson's 'Poor Little Fool', written by 15-year-old Sharon Seeley, who got

Nelson's attention by driving to his house and pretending that her car had broken down.

The second chart-topper was Domenico Modugno's 'Nel blu dipinto di blu' ('In the blue that is painted blue'), popularly known as 'Volare'. Modugno had written the song with Franco Migliacci. The two Italians had planned a trip to the sea together, but as Migliacci waited for Modugno to show up he drank some wine and fell asleep. After dreaming very vividly, he woke to see two reproductions of Marc Chagall paintings that hung on his wall. One was a yellow man suspended in mid-air, while the other showed half of Chagall's face painted blue. Lyrics began to form in Migliacci's mind about a man who dreams of painting himself blue and being able to fly. Later that night he developed the song further with Modugno. Its unveiling came several months later in January 1958 at the San Remo Music Festival. Modugno performed the song with Johnny Dorelli, who was so nervous his partner had to punch him to get him on stage. The song won the festival's competition. Two months later it was Italy's entry for the Eurovision Song Contest, and came third.

But in August it climbed its way to the top of the Billboard Hot 100, staying there for five (non-consecutive) weeks. At the inaugural Grammy Awards in 1959 it won two awards, and remains the only Eurovision song ever to win a Grammy. Modugno used some of his earnings to buy a Ferrari. Unfortunately he then wrote off the car in a crash.

The original Italian version of 'Volare' features in the film *Absolute Beginners*, being played on the radio and sung by David Bowie. The most famous cover version with the English lyrics written by Mitchell Parish is the one by Dean Martin. Gracie Fields wrote her own words for the song, often adapting them to the setting. For instance, on a 1975 episode of Russell Harty's chat show she sang to the audience: 'Over seventy life is divine, now I'm having a wonderful time . . . . I love you, I do, I love you, honest and true.' Slightly more cogent lyrics were used by the fans of Arsenal Football Club for their hero Patrick Vieira: 'He comes from Senegal, he plays for Arsenal.' And then by Manchester United fans after the 1998–9 season, when their team not only took Arsenal's Premier League title and FA Cup but also added the Champions League for good measure: 'He comes from Senegal, last year he won f*** all.'

The discs that didn't: second place in the pop charts

It must be very galling for Midge Ure and the other members of Ultravox that whenever anyone hears 'Vienna' – the band's best-known song, and Single of the Year at the 1981 Brit Awards – the immediate reaction is: 'Oh, that's the record that was kept off the number-one spot by "Shaddap You Face" by Joe Dolce.' The band can't have objected too much to playing second fiddle to 'Woman' by the recently deceased John Lennon, as they did for their first week at number two. But when they were trapped there for a further three weeks by a novelty single sung in cod-Anglo-Italian by an Australian cabaret and pub performer, their patience must have worn thin. It won't have helped that a cover version of 'Shaddap You Face' was released later the same year by Andrew Sachs, as Manuel, the Spanish waiter he played in the sitcom *Fawlty Towers* (the B-side was 'Waiter, There's a Flea in My Soup'). Dolce's version remains the biggest-selling

Australian-produced single ever, with worldwide sales of over 6 million. Perhaps Ultravox can content themselves that 'Vienna' was voted Britain's favourite 'peaked at number two' single in a 2012 poll run, appropriately, by BBC Radio 2.

There was some stiff competition for the title. 'Penny Lane'/'Strawberry Fields Forever', for instance, the Beatles' double-A side that only reached number two in 1967 – their first single since 1963's 'Please Please Me' not to hit the top of the charts (at least not the Record Retailer one, which since 1960 had been the UK's official chart). 'Release Me' by Engelbert Humperdinck was the culprit there. 'The Carnival is Over', a 19th-century Russian folk song covered by The Seekers, was the villain in 1965, blocking The Who's 'My Generation'. This would prove to be the closest the band came to glory – they never had a British number one.

James could only watch in 1991 as their classic 'Sit Down' came second to 'The One and Only' by Chesney Hawkes (it was indeed his sole Top Ten hit). And we can only guess at Noel and Liam Gallagher's reactions when 'Wonderwall' was blocked by 'I Believe'/'Up on the Roof', a double-A side by Robson and Jerome, the actors from the TV series *Soldier Soldier*. This made the Oasis song the third-biggest seller not to top the UK chart, so let's hope the brothers took some comfort in their bank statements. Certainly that was the approach adopted by Don McLean, when his 1972 mega-hit 'American Pie' stuck at number two thanks to 'Son of My Father' by Chicory Tip. McLean always refused to explain the song's lyrics. 'When people ask me what "American Pie" means, I tell them it means I don't ever have to work again if I don't want to.'

A very special sort of frustration exists for artists who just fail to make the number-one spot at Christmas. T. Rex, for instance, saw their 'Jeepster' prevented from being 1971's Christmas number one by Benny Hill's 'Ernie (The Fastest Milkman in the West)'. Kenny Rogers had had the same experience two years earlier when his 'Ruby, Don't Take Your Love to Town' was pipped to the post by Rolf Harris's 'Two Little Boys'. In 1993 Take That's 'Babe' was beaten by Mr Blobby's 'Mr Blobby', and in 2000 'What Makes a Man' by Westlife was kept in the number-two spot by Bob the Builder's 'Can We Fix It?'. It was the boy band's first single not to reach number one. But the biggest indignity has to be that suffered by John Lennon. OK, we know that the boot was sometimes on the other foot – we've seen that Lennon kept 'Vienna' off the top spot, and indeed did the same to Pat Benatar in the album charts (see 'You Better Run', p. 45). But when you've gone to the trouble of being murdered, you certainly don't deserve what happened to the ex-Beatle at Christmas 1980. He was killed on 8 December, sending '(Just Like) Starting Over' (which had peaked at number eight and was on its way back down the charts) to number one. But by the time the Christmas chart came around, Lennon had to play second fiddle – to St Winifred's School Choir with 'There's No One Quite Like Grandma'.

When 'Fairytale of New York' by The Pogues and Kirsty MacColl was held at number two by The Pet Shop Boys' 'Always on My Mind' in 1987, Shane MacGowan – who celebrated his 30th birthday that Christmas Day – said: 'We were beaten by two queens and a drum machine.' The song's video features Matt Dillon as the policeman who escorts MacGowan to his cell. This was filmed at a real New York police station, where the band's drinking started to alarm the cops. Dillon had to assure them that his friend MacGowan would calm down. The lyrics mention 'the boys of the NYPD choir still singing "Galway Bay"'. The NYPD doesn't actually have a choir, but they do have an Irish pipe band, who also feature in the video. They didn't know 'Galway Bay', however, so were instead filmed playing and singing the theme tune to *The Mickey Mouse Club*.

There was a very curious case in 2008, when fans of the late American musician Jeff Buckley spotted that Alexandra Burke, winner of that year's *X Factor* on ITV, had released a single of the Leonard Cohen song 'Hallelujah'. They regarded Buckley's version of the song as definitive, and mounted a campaign to make it the Christmas number one in place of Burke's. They failed, but the track did reach number two. (To make it even more of a payday for Cohen, his own version reached number 36.) This was the first time the same song had occupied the top two positions in the chart since 1957, when Guy Mitchell and Tommy Steele both recorded 'Singing the Blues'.

Another schizophrenic situation occurred in 1984, except this time it was the artist who occupied both spots. George Michael and his Wham! partner Andrew Ridgeley saw their double-A side 'Last Christmas'/'Everything She Wants' denied the Christmas number-one spot by Band Aid's 'Do They Know It's Christmas?'. It is the biggest-selling single not to reach the top spot – which makes Wham!'s decision to donate all their royalties from it to the Band Aid Trust all the more generous.

'Thy choicest gifts in store . . .': second verse of the British national anthem

As with so much of Britain's pomp and tradition, the lyrics of the country's national anthem have no single official version. But according to the royal family's website, the second verse runs as follows:

Thy choicest gifts in store
On her be pleased to pour,
Long may she reign.
May she defend our laws,
And ever give us cause,
To sing with heart and voice,
God save the Queen.

Certainly, this was the second of the two verses sung at the opening ceremony of the 2012 London Olympics. Many sources give the second verse as:

Oh Lord our God arise,
Scatter her enemies,
And make them fall.
Confound their politics,
Frustrate their knavish tricks,
On thee our hopes we fix,
God save us all.

Understandably, this can be seen as somewhat embarrassing, giving off the wrong impressions about Britain's relations with the rest of the world. (It was even more so in the days before 'knavish' replaced 'popish'.) But then there are several other verses (hardly any of which are ever sung), and these could be seen as even more offensive. Billy Connolly, for instance, takes great exception to this:

Lord grant that Marshal Wade
May by thy mighty aid
Victory bring.
May he sedition hush,
And like a torrent rush,
Rebellious Scots to crush.
God save the Queen.

This refers to the army of Field Marshal George Wade, which assembled at Newcastle in 1745 to fight the Scottish uprising led by Bonnie Prince Charlie. As it happened the Scots came down the west coast via Carlisle instead. Connolly's response to the line about crushing rebellious Scots is simple: 'Oh, you bloody think so?' He might be consoled by the fact that one of the many pieces of music cited by scholars as a possible source of the anthem's tune is the old Scottish carol 'Remember O Thou Man'. Others include a 1619 keyboard piece by the English composer John Bull. But whatever the tune's origins, Connolly complains that it is too slow and depressing. He suggests instead that our national anthem should be the theme tune to *The Archers*, with the lyrics 'rum te-tum te-tum te-tum . . .'.

With the Beatles: second album by the Fab Four

Like Doctor Who (see 'Patrick Troughton', p. 35), the Beatles' second album had the misfortune to clear its throat and ask for the world's attention just as JFK was being assassinated. In fact *With the Beatles* was released on the very day the President was killed, 22 November 1963: at least the Timelord didn't appear until over 24 hours later. However, such was the Liverpool band's popularity at the time that the record still sold in huge numbers – indeed it became only the second album to sell a million copies in the UK (after the soundtrack from *South Pacific*).

The famous black and white cover of the Fab Four's heads half in shadow was taken by fashion photographer Robert Freeman, whose other work that year included the first ever Pirelli calendar. He was paid £75 for the album photos, considerably less than the band themselves made from it – although their songwriting earnings weren't as high as with later albums, due to the presence of six cover versions on the fourteen-song LP. One of these was 'Till There Was You', from the 1957 musical *The Music Man*, the only Broadway song the Beatles ever recorded. They'd done an earlier version of it the previous year in an attempt to persuade EMI's George Martin to sign them. He declined – at that stage, though he subsequently changed his mind and the demo disc went on to sell at auction in 2016 for £77,500.

The album features 'Don't Bother Me', George Harrison's first contribution to a Beatles LP, although when it appeared in the band's film *A Hard Day's Night* it was mistakenly credited to Lennon and McCartney. (Frank Sinatra used to make the same error when he sang Harrison's 'Something' in his shows.) 'I Wanna Be Your Man', which really *was* written by John and Paul, had already been recorded by the Rolling Stones and released as their second single on 1 November. The Beatles' own version was sung by Ringo Starr. John Lennon would later dismiss the song: 'It was a throwaway. The only two versions of the song were Ringo's and the Rolling Stones'. That shows how much importance we put on it. We weren't going to give them anything great, right?' But proving just how great the song could have been in the right hands, the art critic Brian Sewell was once recorded breathily reciting the lyrics as a poem. He said they seemed 'rather sexy' to him: 'I don't know what the music's like, but the lyrics suggest highly erotic pillow talk.'

Also on the album was 'All My Loving', which three months later would be the first number the band performed on their legendary *Ed Sullivan Show* appearance in New York. The second was 'Till There Was You', during which captions showed their names as they appeared in turn: John Lennon's was supplemented with 'Sorry Girls, He's Married'. When they appeared on the show the following year (1965), McCartney performed his new song 'Yesterday' solo. He was waiting for the curtains to be pulled back, nervous about appearing without his three bandmates for the first time. The man who was about to handle the curtain asked McCartney if he was nervous. 'No, not really,' he replied, trying to hide his fear. 'You should be,' said the guy, 'there are 73 million people watching.'

The Beatles' first album had been *Please Please Me*. In the UK, at least – in the US the situation was different. The first album over there (released on Vee-Jay Records) was called *Introducing the Beatles*, and contained mostly the material from *Please Please Me*. Then Capitol Records issued *Meet the Beatles*, which roughly equated to the UK's *With the Beatles*. Then Capitol collected together songs from various other sessions the band had done, and called it *The Beatles' Second Album*. Because of the earlier Vee-Jay record, it was actually the Beatles' third album.

Max Martin: second-highest number of Billboard Hot 100 chart-topping singles

You would expect the songwriter who comes second in a list behind Lennon and McCartney to be one of the all-time greats – Irving Berlin, perhaps, or maybe George Gershwin. But what makes this one of the most astonishing seconds of all is the speed with which it has been accomplished. Max Martin (born Karl Martin Sandberg in 1971) is a Swedish songwriter whose 22 Billboard Hot 100 number-one singles have been achieved since 1999. If you have danced or tapped your foot to Britney Spears's 'Baby One More Time', or Maroon 5's 'One More Night', or Taylor Swift's 'Shake It Off', or Justin Timberlake's 'Can't Stop the Feeling', then you have been moved by the work of Max Martin.

After a would-be career as a performer himself, Martin switched to songwriting in the 1990s. He has worked with the Backstreet Boys, Westlife, Celine Dion, Pink, Christina Aguilera, Ariana Grande and Adele, among many others. By 2013 his single sales were estimated to be over 135 million. Of his number-one singles, five entered the Hot 100 at that position. Only the much more famous duo from Liverpool have more chart-toppers. (If you count them separately, John Lennon has 26 and Paul McCartney 32.)

Martin is also much sought after as a producer. He performed this role on most of his 22 number ones – indeed he also holds second place in the chart of most number-one hits for a producer, behind George Martin. One area in which he can claim the top spot is ASCAP (American Society of Composers, Authors and Publishers) Songwriter of the Year Awards – he has ten of them.

In a 2013 interview the American record producer Dr Luke (Lukasz Gottwald) compared himself and Martin: 'If Luke is the Skywalker of pop songcraft, Max is the Obi-Wan: the reclusive master.'

ARTS/CULTURE

◆

James Agate: second castaway on *Desert Island Discs*

When the theatre critic James Agate became the second cast-away on BBC Radio's famous desert island, he didn't have to worry about choosing a luxury or a book – these options weren't open to early guests on the programme. Castaways were provided (as today) with the Bible and the complete works of Shakespeare, but their only requirement was to select eight gramophone records. The programme assumed that they had 'a gramophone and an inexhaustible supply of needles'.

One of Agate's choices on 5 February 1952 (music-hall star Vic Oliver had been the inaugural guest a week earlier) was 'By the Sleepy Lagoon', which happened to be the show's theme tune. Eric Coates had been inspired to write it by the view from the Sussex town of Selsey across the sea to Bognor Regis. The seagull noises were added by the BBC. In 1964 they replaced them with tropical bird calls, on the grounds that these were more accurate for a desert island. You'd think the sort of listener who writes in to the BBC would applaud such accuracy, but no, there were complaints, so the seagulls were reinstated.

Agate, whose nine volumes of diaries were published under the titles *Ego*, *Ego 2*, *Ego 3* and so on, once wrote: 'Long experience has taught me that in England nobody goes to the theatre unless he or she has bronchitis.' He also had form in the 'second' stakes. Meeting the actress Lilian Braithwaite one day at the Savoy Hotel, he said: 'My dear Lilian, I have long wanted to tell you that, in my opinion, you are the second most beautiful woman in London.' No doubt he wanted her to ask who the most beautiful woman in London was, having a witty reply at the ready, but he never got to use it – Braithwaite responded: 'Thank you so much, James. I shall always cherish that, coming from our second-best dramatic critic.'

Squire Bancroft: second actor to be knighted

If you have visited London's Lyceum Theatre (and if you've done that since 19 October 1999 it will have been to watch *The Lion King*), you may or may not have noticed the small plaque, just to the right of the main entrance, recording the fact that Henry Irving (manager of the Lyceum from 1878 to 1902) was the first actor to be knighted. The plaque also mentions that it was while working under Irving at the theatre that Bram Stoker wrote *Dracula*.

Irving's knighthood was awarded in 1895. Just two years later Squire Bancroft became the second knight of the theatre. (An actor called Augustus Harris had received the honour in 1891, but not for services to the stage – by then he was involved in politics, and got his gong for arranging ceremonies during a visit by the Emperor of

Germany.) Bancroft really had been christened 'Squire', which by a happy coincidence is the term for a young man acting as attendant to a knight before becoming a knight himself.

Bancroft and his wife Effie had introduced 'cup-and-saucer drama'. Preceding 'kitchen-sink drama' by over half a century, the phrase denoted the naturalism and realism of the plays' sets and staging. The aim was to attract more middle-class people to the theatre. As part of this, the interiors of theatres themselves were redesigned. Carpets were laid, seats were padded and the area nearest the stage was rechristened the 'stalls' – it had previously been known as the 'pit'.

The only theatre actor to be knighted while actually in a theatre was Frank Benson. A cousin of Basil Rathbone (for many still the defining Sherlock Holmes), his first appearance had been under Irving at the Lyceum (1882, as Paris in *Romeo and Juliet*). Following years of distinguished service to the Shakespearian cause as head of his own theatre company, Benson was knighted in 1916. The ceremony took place in the Royal Box of the Theatre Royal, Drury Lane, after a performance of *Julius Caesar* in which Benson had played the title role. Still in make-up and costume (a toga whose bloodstains denoted the fact he had just been murdered), Benson knelt before King George V for his second brush with a blade that evening.

It's said that Henry Irving's knighthood marked the acceptance of the acting profession into polite British society. This may be so, though it might not have sounded so distinguished had he stuck with his original surname of Brodribb. And his wife Florence didn't agree – one day during a carriage ride she had mocked his profession, asking: 'Are you going on making a fool of yourself like this all your life?' He got out of the carriage, walked off and never saw her again. (They didn't divorce, however, and when he was knighted she called herself Lady Irving.) And on the very next day (25 May 1895) there occurred an event that could be said to have set the theatre back again: Oscar Wilde was found guilty of gross indecency.

Aardwolf: second proper word in the dictionary

Most English dictionaries begin with the indefinite article 'a', but if we take the first 'proper' (that is, multi-letter) word as 'aardvark', the second is 'aardwolf'. This creature lives in Africa, as does the aardvark, which is why both burrow-dwelling animals take their first syllable from the Afrikaans word for 'earth'. They are, however, completely different species. The aardwolf is closer to the hyena. Like the civet, it can emit foul-smelling liquid from its anal glands to ward off aggressors.

The aardwolf can consume 250,000 termites in a single night. (Of course this taste for insects is something it *does* have in common with the aardvark, though the latter animal does so with its unusual tubular teeth, which is why its classification order is *Tubulidentata*.) The oldest recorded aardwolf lived at Frankfurt Zoo, reaching the age of 18 years 11 months.

Exodus: second book of the Bible

In the beginning was the Word, and the Word got so much attention that no one can remember what comes after Genesis. The Bible's second book is in fact Exodus, telling the story of Moses leading the Israelites out of Egypt to the Promised Land. The single most famous event is that of Moses receiving the Ten Commandments from God, written on tablets of stone. In the 1956 movie version of the tale Moses was played by Charlton Heston, while his newborn son Fraser played the infant Moses. These days the parting of the Red Sea would be achieved by CGI, but back then it was a case of filling tanks with water then reversing the film. The hailstones that fell on Rameses' palace were pieces of popcorn painted white, and the sandstorm in the desert was achieved by tying down some Egyptian Air Force planes then starting their engines. The scene in which Moses' people indulge in an orgy during their leader's absence was problematic to film – the actors had to give the impression of outrageous behaviour without actually doing anything the censors would remove. It took so long that one female extra said: 'Who do I have to f*** to get *out* of this movie?'

Changing tone somewhat, we reach Margaret Thatcher. The then Leader of the Opposition referred to the Ten Commandments when Prime Minister Jim Callaghan was said by a colleague to see himself as Moses, leading his people to the Promised Land. Thatcher's speechwriters penned a line for her: 'My message to Moses is, keep taking the tablets.' She summoned the writers and said she wanted to change it to 'keep taking the pills'. Only when the joke was explained to her did she agree to deliver it as written.

John Walter: second editor of *The Times*

Being editor of *The Times* is up there with serving as Archbishop of Canterbury, Governor of the Bank of England, perhaps even Prime Minister. Since the world's most famous newspaper began life in 1785 (known for its first three years as the *Daily Universal Register*), only 22 people have edited it. The second of those, in 1803, was John Walter. It's not hard to see how he got the job: he was the son of the paper's first editor and founder, also called John.

The second Walter worked hard at establishing *The Times's* independence. It opposed the policies of Prime Minister William Pitt the Younger, who retaliated by withdrawing government advertising from it. The paper also suffered a threat to its innovative practice of foreign reporting: its packages containing information were stopped by customs officers at Gravesend. Walter resorted to using smugglers to get his documents into the country. It worked – information from abroad often appeared in *The Times* several days before it was received by government ministers.

Walter's determination to maintain his distance from the government paid off: *The Times* became known as the leading newspaper not just in Britain but in Europe. A key policy was that contributors had to be anonymous. Walter ordered that if two writers who were friends happened to visit the office at the same time they should pass by without acknowledging each other. At least one contributor was unknown even to Walter himself. This man once attended a dinner party where he heard a fellow guest claiming to have written an article he himself had been responsible for. It was a stupid claim to make – anyone familiar with *The Times's* policy would know that either the boaster had never worked for the paper in the first place, or wouldn't be working for it much longer.

Walter also battled against his own employees. In 1810, foreshadowing Rupert Murdoch by a century and a half, he stood up to some *Times* printers who were planning to stop the paper's publication by going on strike (in their case without notice). Walter simply gathered together some workmen from outside the company, and with their help worked for 36 hours straight over a Saturday and Sunday. On the Monday morning the paper appeared as usual.

In 1814 he handed over the reins to the third editor, John Stoddart. But Walter retained an influence, and the two men soon fell out. Stoddart was forced to resign, and started a rival paper called the *New Times*. It never achieved success, Stoddart himself being known as 'Dr Slop'. He was subjected to ridicule in several satires, such as *A Slap at Slop* (1820).

Walter died in 1847. In 1830 he had bought a 5,000-acre estate in Berkshire, where in the 1860s his son (a third John) built a mansion that the architectural historian Nikolaus Pevsner called 'in its brazen way one of the major Victorian monuments of England'. Today it houses a school (Reddam House), and has been featured in such TV dramas as *Endeavour* and *Midsomer Murders*.

Lining up in the shadows: what follows those famous first lines?

'Abide with me,' sings the entire Wembley crowd every year, their voices resonating with pride at the imminent prospect of their teams contesting the FA Cup Final. Then it dawns on them that they don't know the second line: 'Dur-dur-dur-dur-dur,' comes the mass mumble. What *does* appear in the wake of those famous openings in music and literature?

In the case of 'Abide With Me' it is: 'Fast falls the eventide/The darkness deepens/Lord with me abide.' The hymn's lyrics were written in 1847 by the Scottish Anglican Henry Francis Lyte. His eventide was falling particularly quickly at the time: tuberculosis would kill him within just three weeks. The tune is William Henry Monk's 'Eventide', and has captured the imagination of many people down the years. The band on the *Titanic* played it as the ship sank, the nurse Edith Cavell sang it the night before she was executed by the Germans during World War I for helping prisoners to escape, and it was a favourite of King George V, Mahatma Gandhi and Richard Nixon (the latter having it played at his funeral).

'This is the Night Mail crossing the border,/Bringing the cheque and the postal order,' begins W.H. Auden's poem written for the 1936 documentary about the London-to-Scotland mail train. But how does it continue? 'Letters for the rich, letters for the poor/The shop at the corner, the girl next door./Pulling up Beattock, a steady climb:/The gradient's against her, but she's on time.' The reference is to Beattock Summit, the highest point on the West Coast Main Line in Scotland. The film's music was by Benjamin Britten, and it was narrated by the Scottish film-maker John Grierson, who has been credited with coining the word 'documentary'. The poem's rhythm matches that of the train's wheels, though the interior shots of the sorting coach were actually filmed on a studio set. The actors were told to sway from side to side to create the illusion of the train moving.

Turning to literature, we encounter *Anna Karenina*, whose famous first line is: 'Happy families are all alike; every unhappy family is unhappy in its own way.' But what comes next? 'Everything was in confusion in the Oblonskys' house. The wife had discovered that the husband was carrying on an intrigue with a French girl, who had been a governess in their family, and she had announced to her husband that she could not go on living in the same house with him.' Straight into the action, you might say. One of the book's main characters is Konstantin Levin, widely assumed to be based on Lev (Leo) Tolstoy himself: 'Levin' means 'of Lev'. In particular, the character's insistence that his fiancée reads his diary to discover his past sexual encounters is based on the author's arrangement with his own wife-to-be.

Tolstoy has of course inspired many people, not least those who go on to become writers. But a minor episode from his life inspired one particular writer in an unexpected way. A man called Jeremy Baker found, at the age of 35, that his life wasn't going the way he'd hoped it would. Initially disappointed and upset by this, he gradually became interested in how other people's lives had been progressing at that age. Mozart, for instance, had died at 35. Baker ended up writing a wonderful book about the subject, listing the achievements of famous people from history, organised by age. Many of the later entries prove that, as the well-worn saying has it, 'you're never too old'. Well into what we might think of as retirement, people have accomplished incredible things. The book (first published in 1983) is called *Tolstoy's Bicycle*. Why? Because among Baker's many fascinating discoveries was the fact that the famous Russian writer took his first bicycle lesson at the age of 67. The machine on which he did so was donated by the Moscow Society of Velocipede-Lovers.

'It was a dark and stormy night' has become so famous as an opening line that a contest named after its author (Edward Bulwer-Lytton) now exists in which entrants have to write 'the opening sentence to the worst of all possible novels'. This may be because *Paul Clifford* continues: 'the rain fell in torrents – except at occasional intervals, when it was checked by a violent gust of wind which swept up the streets (for it is in London that our scene lies), rattling along the housetops, and fiercely agitating the scanty flame of the lamps that struggled against the darkness.' Certainly the American magazine *Writer's Digest* has called the 1830 novel 'the literary posterchild for bad story starters', though this doesn't bother Snoopy in *Peanuts* – his attempts at novels always begin, 'It was a dark and stormy night'. Maybe Bulwer-Lytton would prefer the rest of us to remember him for coining the phrases 'the Great Unwashed' and 'the pen is mightier than the sword'. He also wrote an early science-fiction novel called *Vril: The Power of the Coming Race*, in which Vril is a source of energy. When the manufacturers of a beef-stock product wanted a name they combined the word with the first two letters of 'bovine' to produce 'Bovril'.

'Some years ago – never mind how long precisely – having little or no money in my purse, and nothing particular to interest me on shore, I thought I would sail about a little and see the watery part of the world.' Could you guess which novel this sentence comes from? Perhaps the sailing reference is a clue, but the line certainly isn't as famous as the one before it: 'Call me Ishmael.' Herman Melville's *Moby Dick* was published in 1851, the whale's name partly inspired by

Mocha Dick, an albino sperm whale that lived near Mocha Island off the coast of Chile. An account of the creature had appeared in the magazine *The Knickerbocker* in 1839. Gregory Peck played Captain Ahab in the 1956 movie version, then portrayed Father Mapple in the 1998 version – his final screen performance. By that time the musician Moby had achieved worldwide dominance of the pop charts, his name derived from the fact that he (Richard Melville Hall) is Herman Melville's great-great-great-grand-nephew.

But the ultimate first line, the one you always see in quizzes, is: 'It was a bright cold day in April, and the clocks were striking thirteen.' How does *1984* (working title: *The Last Man in Europe*) continue? 'Winston Smith, his chin nuzzled into his breast in an effort to escape the vile wind, slipped quickly through the glass doors of Victory Mansions, though not quickly enough to prevent a swirl of gritty dust from entering along with him.' The inspiration for Victory Mansions, home to our anti-hero, was Langford Court in London's St John's Wood. George Orwell and his wife lived here while the author was working for the BBC. Were it not for the trees on the right of the picture, you would be able to see Langford Court on the famous 'zebra crossing' cover of the Beatles' album *Abbey Road*.

Groundhog Day: the ultimate second (and third, fourth, fifth . . .)

On 8 August 2017, Bill Murray, star of the 1993 movie *Groundhog Day*, attended a performance of a musical based on the film at the August Wilson Theatre on Broadway,

New York. The following night he returned to watch the show for a second time. Dear old Bill, celebrating the joke behind the film (his character being forced to live the same day again and again and again). You'd think he'd had enough of groundhogs – during filming he was bitten twice by the creature playing Punxsutawney Phil, the groundhog who, in the old Pennsylvania tradition, emerges from his burrow on 2 February and predicts whether spring is about to arrive. It 'works' by the groundhog either seeing or failing to see his shadow: the former (caused by sunny weather) makes him retreat into his den, forecasting six more weeks of winter, while the latter (caused by an absence of sun) announces that spring is here early. The prediction is therefore the opposite of the weather on the day. Since 1887 the groundhog's success rate is 39 per cent.

SPORT

◆

John Landy: second man to run a sub-four-minute mile

On 21 June 1954, just a few weeks after Roger Bannister had broken the four-minute barrier for the mile, the Australian athlete John Landy repeated the feat. In fact his time that day in Turku, Finland, was faster than that of the more famous man. It set a record that would last for three years: three minutes, 57.9 seconds.

Landy ran another sub-four-minute mile later the same year, when he finished second in the British Empire and Commonwealth Games in Vancouver. First place went to . . . Roger Bannister. Over 100 million people listened to the radio commentary of the 'Miracle Mile'. On the last bend Landy looked over his left shoulder, thereby missing Bannister passing him on the right. A statue of this moment now stands in the Canadian city. Landy said that Lot's wife had been turned into a pillar of salt for looking back, but he was turned into bronze.

At the 1956 Melbourne Olympics, Landy stopped during the final of the 1,500 metres to check on Ron Clarke, who had fallen while leading the race. Incredibly, after setting off again, he made up the large deficit that resulted from this sporting act and won the gold medal.

At the Olympic Games eight years earlier, in London, Bannister's speed had saved the home nation's blushes. Just minutes before the opening ceremony was due to begin someone realised that Britain didn't have a flag to march under: the *chef de mission* had left it in the boot of his car. His teenage assistant – Bannister – was sent to get it, in a Jeep driven by an army sergeant. Bannister himself kept sounding the horn to get them through the traffic. 'We managed to find the car,' he said, 'but I didn't have a key, so I smashed the window. The traffic was so heavy going back that I had to get out and run, and I only arrived with seconds to spare. If you look at the video of the parade, you will notice that the British flag is smaller than all the others.'

George Camsell: second-highest total of league goals in a single season

Dixie Dean's total of 60 goals in Everton's 1927–8 campaign is only one more than Camsell's haul for Middlesbrough the previous season. The former miner's total of 59 included nine hat-tricks. Camsell was a serial seconder: his feat of scoring in nine consecutive games for England would be the record were it not for Steve Bloomer, who scored in ten. Like Camsell, Bloomer had scored on his debut (1895) and carried on. But Camsell never got the chance to equal the tally – he only ever played nine matches for England, scoring in all of them. At least if he was around today he could console himself with the fact that those international goals – 18 of them – still give him the record for the highest goals-to-games ratio of any man ever to play more than once for England. His overall tally for club and country could have been even higher had he taken penalties – but after missing one early in his career he refused to take any more.

After retiring, Camsell worked for Middlesbrough as a scout. One of the players he discovered was a young man called Brian Clough.

Steve Daley: second million-pound footballer

Seven months after Trevor Francis grabbed the headlines in the first seven-figure transfer, Daley moved from Wolves to Manchester City. His own website now bills him as the 'first £1,437,500' footballer, though headlines of the time called him the 'Million Pound Misfit' and the 'White Elephant Man'. A 2001 *Observer* article described the move as 'the biggest waste of money in football history'.

Manchester City's manager and chairman were left arguing about who had inflated the fee so much, and just 20 months later Daley was sold to US club the Seattle Sounders for £300,000.

Peter Shilton: second-highest number of appearances at the original Wembley Stadium

By turning out beneath the famous twin towers 58 times (for England and his various clubs), goalkeeper Peter Shilton set a record that only Tony Adams (England and Arsenal) managed to beat. On one of those 60 occasions Adams managed to break a team-mate's arm: during the celebrations following their 1993 League Cup Final victory over Sheffield Wednesday, Adams lifted Steve Morrow in triumph, only to see the defender disappear over his shoulder and land heavily.

Similarly, Shilton's most famous match at Wembley is remembered for the wrong reasons. Certainly by the man himself – he says that the goal he conceded against Poland in 1973, which effectively cost England their place in the following year's World Cup Finals, was his only mistake in 125 international appearances. England had to win the match, and did indeed score, Allan Clarke slotting home a penalty. The match became legendary for the incredible number of chances squandered by the home side, thanks partly to the efforts of the Polish goalkeeper Jan Tomaszewski, who'd been called a 'clown' by Brian Clough in the pre-match TV build-up.

But had Shilton not let in a goal by Jan Domarski, the 1–0 scoreline would have been enough. Domarski's shot wasn't that well hit, but Shilton tried to make 'the perfect save', catching the ball rather than merely parrying it away. As a result he was out of position, and the shot found its way into the net.

Even more famous than this, however, is what happened to Shilton on 22 June 1986 in Mexico's Estadio Azteca. Facing Argentina in the quarter-finals of the World Cup, England had managed to reach half-time without conceding a goal. But six minutes into the second half the opposition's star player, Diego Maradona, went up for a ball against Shilton. Despite being 5 feet 5 inches compared to Shilton's 6 feet 1 inch, Maradona still managed to get the ball into the net.

The answer to this riddle was, of course, that he had punched it. Shilton and his England colleagues instantly pointed this out to the referee. Meanwhile Maradona 'was waiting for my team-mates to embrace me, and no one came . . . I told them: "Come and hug me, or the referee isn't going to allow it."' They did, he did and the goal stood.

Alf Ramsey: second manager of the England football team

Ramsey had played under the first manager, Walter Winterbottom, during England's first-ever World Cup (Brazil in 1950). Before this the English FA had considered that entering a team into the competition was beneath them. Ramsey's last international match as a player – the famous 6–3 loss to Hungary in 1953 – was itself a second: the only other nation to beat England in England had been the Republic of Ireland in 1949. As was his first-ever professional match, in 1946 for Southampton: it was only the second senior match he'd ever attended (the first being the West Ham–Arsenal encounter he'd watched as a schoolboy).

Ramsey took over from his old boss in 1963, and unlike Winterbottom was given complete control of squad selection. (His predecessor had had his squads chosen for him by an FA committee.) Of course his World Cup triumph of 1966 cemented his place in the history books, but he never lost his strange insecurities. He always knocked two years off his age, something he'd first done to improve his chances of becoming a professional, reasoning that World War II had interrupted his career in its prime. He carried on lying in his autobiography and even to *Who's Who*: it was only when he was knighted and included in Debrett's that he felt he had to tell the truth.

There were rumours that Ramsey had Romany blood – and they were rumours he didn't like. He was furious when Bobby Moore saw some Romany caravans and joked that the manager should 'drop in to see his relatives'. He was also livid when Moore and Jimmy Greaves mocked his 'pseudo-posh' accent on the team bus (Ramsey was from Dagenham), and when the pair laughed at him for pronouncing Sean Connery's first name as 'Seen' ('Now I've *seen* everything,' said Moore). Ramsey said he would 'win the World Cup without those two bastards'. In the event Moore captained the side to victory, but after an early injury Greaves was left out of the final.

1873: second FA Cup Final

It's hard now to imagine people leaving the FA Cup Final early to watch the Boat Race, but that's exactly what happened on 29 March 1873. The match was scheduled for the same day as the race, so the organisers moved it from the previous year's venue (the Kennington Oval) to the Lillie Bridge sports ground in west London, near the stretch of the Thames on which the famous event took place. They even played it in the morning, so people could watch both contests. But only 3,000 people turned up, and many of those missed the end so they could head to the Thames.

Presumably these were Cambridge supporters: one of the teams in the Cup Final was Oxford University. They were up against defending champions Wanderers FC, who, in line with the original notion of a 'challenge cup', had received a bye straight through to the final. (In fact, this would be the only time the rule was used.) Wanderers were so called because they had no ground of their own. Their first match under this name had been in 1864 against the No Names Club of Kilburn, whose moniker may have derived from the fact that their founder worked in stockbroking, where investors are known as 'names'.

One of Oxford's players was Walpole Vidal, known as the 'Prince of Dribblers'. Back then the team that had just scored kicked off at the restart – this had once allowed Vidal to score a hat-trick without the other team touching the ball. He had played in the first FA Cup Final the previous year, for Wanderers, and had set up the only goal of the match, allowing Morton Betts to complete a simple tap-in. But this year, having left Westminster School and progressed to university, he was up against his old team.

Wanderers boasted the first-ever foreign player to appear in an FA Cup Final, the American novelist and librettist Julian Sturgis. Their captain, Arthur Kinnaird, opened the scoring after 27 minutes, and in a desperate attempt to fight back Oxford dispensed with their goalkeeper, Andrew Louch, allowing him to play upfield. This backfired when Charles Wollaston scored again for Wanderers, who won 2–0. As was customary then the trophy wasn't presented on the day, but at the team's annual dinner later in the year.

Wanderers' two scorers that day went on to become the first players to win five FA Cups, a feat that wouldn't be bettered until Ashley Cole's sixth victory in 2010. Two of Kinnaird's victories were for Old Etonians, and indeed his tally of nine appearances in the final remains a record.

Meanwhile, that day in 1873, Oxford's disappointment continued in the afternoon – they lost the Boat Race.

1934: second football World Cup

Arguments between bureaucrats, violent play on the field and the glorification of fascism: welcome to football's golden age.

If the controversies surrounding recent World Cups have had you longing for a return to a simpler time when friendly amateurism ruled the day, a look at the 1934 World Cup should remove the rosy tint from your glasses. FIFA's executive committee met no fewer than eight times before confirming Italy as hosts, at which point defending champions Uruguay refused to take part. Several European nations had refused to travel to South America for the first World Cup in 1930 (hosted by Uruguay themselves), so the champions weren't going to make the return trip now. It's still the only World Cup in which the title holders didn't take part. (It's also the only one for which the host nation had to qualify.) The British teams also declined to enter. The FA's Charles Sutcliffe explained that England, Scotland, Wales and Ireland had 'quite enough to do in their own International Championship, which seems to me a far better World Championship than the one to be staged in Rome'.

The last qualifying match took place only three days before the tournament proper, the United States edging out Mexico. Egypt became the first team from Africa to take part – they wouldn't qualify again until the World Cup

returned to Italy in 1990. The group stages used in the first
World Cup were abandoned in favour of a straight knock-
out tournament. The hosts lost no time in dispatching the
US 7–1, the *New York Times* correspondent admitting that
it would have been worse but for the fine goalkeeping of
Chicago's Julius Hjulian. Argentina lost to Sweden – arguments within the South American side meant that not one
member of their team which had reached the final in 1930
appeared this time.

Italy's next match was against Spain. Both teams played
dirty: Italy's Mario Pizziolo had his leg broken (he never
played for the national team again), while Spanish goalkeeper Ricardo Zamora was so badly hurt that he couldn't take
part in the replay that followed the 1–1 draw. This match
(the first-ever World Cup replay) was a similar affair: three
Spaniards had to leave the field, and Italy won 1–0. There
were rumours (as throughout the tournament) that pressure
had been placed on the referee to favour Italy – Benito Mussolini was keen to use the tournament as a way of promoting
himself and his party. (The Italian side had greeted him with
fascist salutes.) Certainly one of the decisions in this match
was strange: the referee disallowed a Spanish goal, recalling
the play to award them a free kick.

Having beaten Austria in the semi-finals, Italy faced
Czechoslovakia in the final, which was held at the Stadium
of the National Fascist Party in Rome. The temperature was
nudging 40 degrees Celsius, and Mussolini was there to
present the trophy. Luis Monti, playing for Italy, had played
for the losing Argentinian team in the 1930 final: he remains
the only man to appear in two World Cup Finals for different countries. Also appearing for the home side was the man

after whom the San Siro Stadium in his native Milan is now named – it's officially the Stadio Giuseppe Meazza.

Czechoslovakia scored first, just over halfway through the second half, but ten minutes later Italy equalised to take the match into extra time. Angelo Schiavio scored the winner, allowing captain Gianpiero Combi to receive the Jules Rimet trophy from Mussolini. Only Combi's fellow Italian Dino Zoff (1982), Spain's Iker Casillas (2010) and France's Hugo Lloris (2018) have repeated the feat of captaining the World Cup champions from the goalmouth.

Scotland versus Wales: second-oldest fixture in international football

Starting in 1872, Scotland had played five matches against England by the time a third team appeared on the international football scene. On 25 March 1876, at Hamilton Crescent in Partick, Scotland hosted Wales. The visitors, who had had to appeal for public donations to pay their travel costs, were almost all from the north of Wales. In the long and dishonourable tradition of sporting groups arguing more between themselves than with the opposition, C. C. Chambers, the captain of Swansea, objected to the bias, writing that 'there must be some sort of error ... I shall be happy to produce from these parts a team that shall hold their own against any team from North Wales.'

There was huge interest in the fixture, a crowd of 17,000 cramming into the ground, with many more standing on the roofs of parked horse-buses to see over them. (During the first half a fence collapsed, allowing another 100 people to enter the ground.) Wales played in white shirts with the Prince of Wales feathers on them, while Scotland wore blue. To allow spectators to identify individual players more easily each man wore socks of a different colour, the list being printed in the match programme.

Both teams adopted a 2-2-6 formation, and when the home captain, Charles Campbell, won the toss he elected to play downhill but into the sun. The result was never in doubt: the score at half-time was only 1–0 to Scotland, but in the second half they added another three goals. One of the scorers, James Lang, had only one eye, having lost the other in a shipyard accident at Clydebank. The Scottish inside left, Moses McNeil, had four years earlier founded Rangers FC, taking the name from a book about English rugby.

Wales's left back was Llewelyn Kenrick, the man who had organised the match and selected the Welsh team. He was also in the process of creating the Welsh Football Association. An initial meeting had been held the previous month, and in May there would be another. This took place at the Wynnstay Arms Hotel in Ruabon. One of the decisions taken was to change the provisional name of 'Cambrian Football Association' to 'the Football Association of Wales'. This and further such crucial discussions continued for so long, and resulted in such disagreement, that a policeman eventually appeared, reminding those present that the hotel's closing time had passed and ordering them to disband. He hadn't, however, reckoned on one of them being Sir Watkin Williams-Wynn, who as well as sitting as the local Member of Parliament was also a Justice of the Peace. He opened up the court (not difficult – it was next door), extended the hotel's licensing hours and thereby allowed the meeting to continue.

Terry Neill: second player to take a penalty in an English football shoot-out

It seems deeply unfair that the first player in English football to step up to the spot in a penalty shoot-out was not – as it might well have been, given that the shoot-out could have come along at any time – a journeyman pro from the lower leagues, but George Best. The kudos from starring in this pub fact, the glory that could have burnished an otherwise unremarkable and un-noted career, was stolen by the most famous player of his (or indeed any) generation. Of all firsts, this has to be the greediest.

The second player to take a penalty that balmy summer night of Wednesday 5 August 1970 was Terry Neill. The occasion was a semi-final of the Watney Cup, a short-lived pre-season competition which gathered together the previous season's two highest-scoring teams from each of the four divisions (excluding those who had been promoted or achieved a European competition place). The competition was the first in English football to be sponsored, and given players' lifestyles back then it was fitting that the firm chosen was a brewery. Watney was famous for its Party Seven, a tin holding said number of pints of bitter. The Steve Coogan character Paul Calf fondly remembered that 'one of those would last me all the way to the pub'.

The venue was Boothferry Park, home to Hull City,

whose supporters would one day come to know it as 'Fer Ark' when the club's financial state meant its illuminated sign only had six working letters left. The visitors were Manchester United, and the attendance figure of 34,007 gave the fixture its nickname 'the James Bond game'. The score at full time was 1–1, meaning the new-fangled penalty shoot-out came into play. Best opened the scoring for Man Utd, leaving his Northern Ireland team-mate Terry Neill to take the first penalty for Hull City. Neill was the club's player-manager, having joined them the previous month from Arsenal, where in 1962 he had been (at 20 years and 102 days) the club's youngest-ever captain, a record he still holds. Neill duly scored. Brian Kidd (United) and Ian Butler (Hull) made it 2–2, before Bobby Charlton (United) and Chris Simpkin (Hull) brought the score to 3–3.

Then up stepped another United star, Denis Law, who promptly became the first player ever to miss a penalty in a shoot-out. It didn't take long for the second player to miss – Hull's Ken Wagstaff with the very next attempt, meaning the score remained level. Willie Morgan put United 4–3 ahead, meaning that if Hull missed they would lose. The player in question was none other than the team's goalkeeper, Ian McKechnie, who had just saved from Denis Law. Sadly his heroics came to an end: he hit the bar, thereby putting his team out of the Cup. Unsurprisingly this is what he's remembered for by Hull City fans. That and the oranges they threw into his goalmouth at home matches after he was seen eating one during a training session. Some of the oranges had good-luck messages – and even telephone numbers – attached to them. One fan was arrested for throwing an orange at McKechnie during an away match against

Sheffield United: the Sheffield police weren't aware of the tradition, and McKechnie had to write to them in the fan's defence.

Terry Neil must have gained some comfort a few days later when Manchester United lost in the Watney Cup Final to Derby County (Brian Clough's first-ever trophy as a manager). The penalty shoot-out, meanwhile, has gone on to play a long and dramatic role in the history of football. Not just in England: the final of the 1973 Campeonato Paulista (the top-flight competition in the Brazilian state of São Paulo) went to a shoot-out. After six kicks Santos were leading Portuguesa 2–0. With two kicks left to each team, Portuguesa could still have pulled level, but the referee mistakenly declared Santos the winners. Instead of protesting, the Portuguesa manager quickly got his team out of the stadium, so that the shoot-out couldn't resume if the error was discovered – he reasoned that a replayed match gave them a better chance of victory than having to score both penalties and save both of Santos's. But Santos objected to a replay, so the first match was annulled and the two teams were declared joint champions.

Adam Voges: second-highest Test cricket average of all time

No one will ever come close to Don Bradman's famous Test average of 99.94. Even finishing your career with an average in the low sixties is almost unheard of. Among the players who have done it, Adam Voges is the nearest to Bradman, on 61.87.

Voges had previously made headlines in the shorter forms of the game: in just his second ING Cup 50-over match for Western Australia he hit a six that connected with the small sponsor's sign at the deep-mid-wicket boundary, thereby earning himself Aus $50,000. And in a 2009 T20 game for Australia against New Zealand he took a miraculous catch. Clutching the ball just inside the boundary, he began to wobble. Knowing he was about to step over the line, he threw the ball into the air, allowing himself to catch it again after diving back in from outside the rope.

The following month he left a tour of South Africa to return home for his wedding. 'It's a big thing to give up an opportunity to play for Australia,' he said. 'But I guess you only get married once and that's important to me and a decision I've made and one that I'm comfortable with.' In the end his relaxed attitude paid dividends: in June 2015, at the age of 35, he finally made his Test debut. He marked the occasion – against the West Indies in Dominica – by scoring a century, the oldest man ever to do so in his first Test. By the time he played his 20th and last Test, in November 2016, he had scored five centuries. These included consecutive knocks of 269 not out, 106 not out and 239, making a total between dismissals of 614. This broke Sachin Tendulkar's record of 497. When Voges reached 172 in that knock of 239 his average passed 100, though when he was out it dropped back to a mere 97.46. One of his partners in the innings, Usman Khawaja, said that he might start calling his colleague 'Sir Voges' in a nod to Bradman, thereby showing great respect (if an incomplete understanding of how knights are addressed).

For many years the number-two position was held by

South Africa's Graeme Pollock, with his Test average of 60.97. Like Voges he played relatively few matches – just 23, a cruel consequence of South Africa's sporting isolation during the years of apartheid. But all except one of those matches were against England or Australia, the strongest sides of the era.

At school in Port Elizabeth he had attracted the nickname 'Little Dog'. This was because his older brother Peter had a high-pitched voice, in which his LBW appeals sounded like a dog barking: he became 'Big Dog' and Graeme 'Little Dog'. Playing at home, Peter would let his younger brother bat first, but then Graeme would refuse to accept when he was out. 'That's how I became the bowler,' said Peter, 'and he the batsman.'

The practice paid off. Aged just nine, Graeme scored 117 not out in a school match. He had to placate the opposition bowlers by running into the neighbouring cemetery and retrieving his own sixes. When he played for his local club side everyone came to watch, parking their cars all the way round the boundary. The batsman who usually went in after him said: 'I would walk to the crease with cars hooting to acknowledge another great Pollock innings. As I took guard the engines would start up. And by the time I scored my first run, the ground was once again empty.'

Pollock's performance on the international scene was just as emphatic. At 19, in the 1963–4 series against Australia, he became the youngest South African to score a Test century (he still is). Had politics not intervened there would have been many more than those 23 matches. As it is, Pollock understands why his country was excluded by the other cricketing nations. In 1971, in an exhibition match to mark the tenth anniversary of the Republic of South Africa, he and the other players walked off after just one ball as a protest against the Republic's racial discrimination.

One player who didn't forget this second was the guy in first place. Don Bradman described Pollock (along with Garry Sobers) as the best left-handed batsman he ever saw. He'd always enjoyed watching him at the crease. 'Next time you decide to play like that,' he told Graeme after that first Test century, 'send me a telegram.'

Australia versus England: second-ever Test match

As the teams took to the ground at Melbourne on 31 March 1877, expectations were that Australia would repeat their victory of a fortnight earlier in the first Test match. In fact England played so well there were rumours that their previous poor performance had been a deliberate attempt to increase the odds on them for this match. It wasn't the only rumour of betting irregularity the tour had seen.

The two matches, which were later deemed to be the first-ever Tests (though they are not part of the Ashes, which began five years later), both took place at the Melbourne Cricket Club. The home team were captained by Dave Gregory, a father of 16 who was described by one modern writer as looking like 'an Old Testament prophet not long out of training college'. England were captained by James Lillywhite, one of several members of the famous cricketing family who also established the Piccadilly Circus sports goods store that still bears their name. (Their No. 5 football, adopted by the FA, was the precursor of the ball used today.)

Lillywhite's team was composed of professionals – a rival tour including amateurs and led by Fred Grace (W.G.'s younger brother) had fallen through. It was felt that this side – possibly including W.G. himself – would have been stronger. Lillywhite's team didn't even have a specialist wicket-keeper, the man selected (Ted Pooley) having been arrested earlier in the tour in New Zealand. A bookmaker had offered 20–1 to anyone predicting a batsman's exact score. Pooley put a shilling on each batsman making 0, and when 11 of them scored ducks he claimed his £9 15s. The bookmaker refused to pay up, and Pooley assaulted him. (He was a hard man: he once lost three of his teeth while keeping wicket, a witness saying: 'I heard that ball strike you as if it had hit a brick wall.') Before you assume that this is a case of a player betting on a match in which he was playing, think again: Pooley was injured. Instead of playing he was umpiring.

One of the England players was James Southerton, whose appearance in the first match at the age of 49 years 119 days gives him the title of oldest Test debutant to this day. (There have still only been 13 debutants in their forties, the most recent being South Africa's Oman Henry in 1992.) Australia were boosted by the appearance of star players Fred Spofforth (the 'Demon Bowler') and wicket-keeper Billy Murdoch. The latter had been left out of the side for the first Test, prompting the former to boycott the match in protest. This was seen as big-headed for a player of 23 – as someone put it at the time, 'this modest gentleman was left out'.

Australia won the toss and batted first, but played badly and were all out for 122 in 112.1 four-ball overs. Top-scoring with 31 was Billy Midwinter, who would go on to play four Tests for England before returning to the Australian side (the only Test player ever to – as Churchill would have put it – rat and then re-rat). By the close of play England had also lost wickets, finishing at 7 for 2, but on the second day they rallied to make 261 all out. Australia batted better in their second innings, finishing the third day on 207 for 7 and eventually making 259 to leave England requiring 121. This they did with four wickets in hand, levelling the two-match series.

Test cricket might have begun much sooner had it not been for the French Revolution. In 1789 a group led by John Sackville, the 3rd Duke of Dorset (and recently Britain's Ambassador in Paris), assembled at Dover ready for a tour of France, only to hear that its capital was now gripped by violent revolt. They thought better of making the trip. So those two matches in Melbourne opened the record books. Charles Bannerman's 165 in Australia's 245 during the first Test is still the highest percentage of a team total scored by an individual batsman (67.34 per cent; second place goes to Michael Slater's 66.84 per cent, with 123 out of Australia's 184 against England at Sydney in 1999). And as well as being the oldest debutant, James Southerton would go on to become the first Test cricketer to die, when he succumbed to pleurisy just a few months after retiring from the game in 1880.

Ravi Shastri: second batsman to hit six sixes in an over

The perfect over for a batsman – hitting every ball for six – is the ultimate nightmare for a bowler. In January 1985, 17 years after Garry Sobers had inflicted it on Glamorgan's Malcolm Nash, the Indian great Ravi Shastri became the second man to achieve the feat.

He was playing for Bombay in a Ranji Trophy match against Baroda, at the sporting ground responsible for more schoolboy sniggers than any other, the Wankhede Stadium. The match had started with some off-field drama, when Bombay captain Sunil Gavaskar dropped Dilip Vengsarkar from the team for being late. Vengsarkar was furious: he had only arrived in Bombay late the previous night, after playing in a benefit match elsewhere, and thought he had Gavaskar's permission to get to the ground later than his team-mates. Watching all this with interest was 22-year-old Ravi Shastri, who had been dropped from the previous match by Gavaskar for similar reasons. This time he had been on the same late flight as Vengsarkar, but had been careful to arrive on time.

Both sides declared their first innings with scores of over 300. On the third day, Shastri made his way to the middle during Bombay's second innings. Having started his Test career at number ten in the order, he had worked his way up to become an opener for the national side. He sometimes annoyed the crowd by scoring slowly – indeed only ten days earlier he had taken 455 minutes and 357 balls to score 111 against England at Calcutta. But now, batting at number six for Bombay, he was a man transformed. His first 50 took just 42 balls, and he reached his century in a further 38.

Then, on 147, he faced the first ball of an over from left-arm spinner Tilak Raj. He hit it straight back down the ground for six. The next ball sailed over wide long-on in its journey to the same fate. As did the next. But not the fourth ball – Shastri hit that over mid-wicket. Two more straight hits and he had equalled Sobers's achievement, taking his score to 183. The only journalist present at both matches,

Dicky Rutnagur, ranked the West Indian's over as greater because Malcolm Nash was a frontline bowler, whereas Tilak Raj wasn't. But others pointed out that Swansea, where Sobers hit his six sixes, was a much smaller ground than the Wankhede.

Shastri's big hitting continued for a few more minutes: his first hundred having taken 80 balls, his second took just 43, the fastest double century in the history of first-class cricket. (It would be 2016 before Glamorgan's Aneurin Donald equalled this 123-ball record.) Bombay declared with Shastri on 200 not out. Baroda finished on 81 for 7, the match drawn.

A handful of batsmen have scored six sixes in an over since then, including Herschelle Gibbs for South Africa during the 2007 World Cup. But one second that will almost certainly never occur is hitting a six over the pavilion at Lord's. Albert Trott (a distant ancestor of the modern England player Jonathan Trott) managed it while playing for the MCC against Australia in 1899. Several Middlesex players tried to achieve it for a publicity video in 2016. None of them succeeded.

Vijay Merchant: second-highest first-class batting average of all time

Perhaps inevitably, as well as topping the Test averages, Don Bradman also has the highest first-class average of any batsman ever (a paltry 95.14, compared to 99.94 in Tests). In second place, on 71.64, is the Indian cricketer Vijay Merchant. Born in 1911 in what was then Bombay, he excelled as a school batsman while at Sydenham College. This form continued into domestic cricket, and during England's 1933 tour of India Merchant faced the visitors for a Bombay Presidency side. During the second innings he was hit on the chin by a ball from the Essex fast bowler Stan Nichols. Led from the field, he was attended to by an English doctor who was watching the match. The doctor stitched up the wound and refused to let Merchant see it in a mirror, sending him back onto the field to resume his innings. Merchant was left with a scar, but the incident cured his fear of fast bowling. He was then selected for the Tests against England, the first Tests ever held in India.

His international career would go on to span 18 years, but as six of those saw World War II, and illness caused him to miss tours to Australia and the West Indies, he only played ten matches. The last was against England at Delhi in 1951, where he made 154, his highest Test score. A shoulder injury he sustained while fielding brought about the end of his career. But while it had lasted Merchant had impressed even the greats of the game. After India's 1936 tour of England, C.B. Fry exclaimed – as men like C.B. Fry could in those days – 'Let us paint him white and take him with us to Australia as an opener.' The English climate wasn't easy for Merchant: on India's 1946 tour a wet summer helped him lose a stone in weight. But it didn't stop him from scoring 2,385 runs at an average of 74.

His success was partly down to his habit of having his innings filmed. After play he would study the footage carefully. Merchant was never a flamboyant player – in fact his conservative style helped establish the tradition known as the Bombay School of Batsmanship, in which technique and temperament were more valued than flashy stroke play.

Nevertheless Merchant's innings could be entertaining: one writer recorded that he 'delights onlookers by the neat skill of his glances and general placing to leg'. His average in the Ranji Trophy (India's domestic first-class championship) was even higher than his overall figure – 98.75 over 47 innings. He was one of Wisden's five Cricketers of the Year in 1937, and remains the oldest Indian player to score a Test century – that 154 in his final match, at the age of 40 years 21 days. His eleven first-class double centuries were the most by any Indian batsman until Cheteshwar Pujara scored his twelfth in 2017. All of this in the days of uncovered wickets.

In retirement Merchant became a cricket administrator and selector, as well as hosting a programme on All India Radio. 'Indeed,' wrote someone long after Merchant's death, 'even Mumbaikars who have succumbed to the spicy flavours of FM and psychedelic charms of MTV turn misty-eyed over the good old days of "Cricket with Vijay Merchant".'

Anil Kumble: second bowler to take all ten wickets in a Test innings

The second and final match of India's 1999 home series against Pakistan was the 1,443rd Test match ever played. In the preceding 1,442, there had only been one instance of a bowler taking all ten wickets in an innings: Jim Laker for England against Australia in 1956. India's fans needed something to cheer in Delhi – their defeat in the first match had reduced star player Sachin Tendulkar to tears – but they didn't know just how much there would be to applaud.

The match took place at the Feroz Shah Kotla ground

(the second-oldest international cricket stadium in India, after Kolkata's Eden Gardens). The pitch had needed repairing after Hindu extremists opposed to the tour (Pakistan's first to India in 12 years) had vandalised it. The host nation played well, setting Pakistan an unlikely 420 to win in the final innings. The visitors made a good start, openers Saeed Anwar and Shahid Afridi putting on 101. Of those runs 27 were scored off 28-year-old computer engineer Anil Kumble. His six overs from the Pavilion Stand End did little justice to his nickname of 'Miser', earned because he gave away so few runs. His other nickname was Jumbo, partly because he bowled very fast for a leg-spinner, partly because his feet were so big.

After lunch, captain Mohammad Azharuddin switched Kumble to the Pavilion End. This made an instant difference: in the first over Afridi edged the ball to wicket-keeper Nayan Mongia. This was the umpire's verdict at least – replays left considerable doubt as to whether Afridi had made contact. Either way, there was little argument over Kumble's next wicket, which came the very next ball when Ijaz Ahmed was given out LBW. These two dismissals might not have been solely due to the change of end. Before the over began, Sachin Tendulkar had come across from mid-on and said to Kumble: 'Let me change your luck – let me give your cap and sweater to the umpire.' This he did. From then on, whenever a stand looked like developing the pair would repeat the move. Every time Tendulkar handed over the cap and sweater, a wicket would fall. By tea Pakistan had lost six wickets, all to Kumble.

But even when he took the next wicket after the break, the bowler still hadn't considered the possibility of getting the whole side out. He was simply trying to beat his previous best Test figures of seven for 49. 'You don't think about these things, you are too involved in the action, in trying to win the game for the team, to worry about stuff like this.' It was only when he took the eighth and ninth wickets with the last two balls of his 26th over that the thought occurred – not just to Kumble but to Javagal Srinath, the bowler at the other end. 'I was just hoping that I didn't get a wicket,' he said later. 'I was praying that the batsman didn't get out, even by mistake.' To minimise the chances he aimed well away from the stumps, conceding two wides in the process. Waqar Younis took a heave at one of the deliveries, sending the ball high towards long leg. Despite the cries of his Indian team-mates not to take the catch, fielder Sadagoppan Ramesh made an effort to do so. Fortunately for Kumble he failed. (Srinath made plain to Ramesh his feeling that he shouldn't even have tried.) Kumble appreciated Srinath's gesture – after all, he had done the same himself for Kapil Dev in 1994, when Dev was trying to beat Richard Hadlee's record Test haul of 431 wickets. He 'aimed at the sixth stump', so allowing Dev to get the last batsman out.

So Kumble began his 27th over once more on a hat-trick. Wasim Akram saw off the first ball to deny him that achievement. 'You can't get a hat-trick and ten wickets,' he would say later. 'I think that is asking for too much.' But Kumble was still keen to finish things off in this over: 'Otherwise it would have been embarrassing for Sree [Srinath] to bowl a similar over again.' Two balls later Akram nicked the ball to short leg, where V.V.S. Laxman took a fine catch to complete the innings. India had won by 212 runs, and Kumble had made history. He grabbed a stump from the bowler's end, while his team-mate Venkatesh Prasad quietly pocketed the ball: he would give it to Kumble later. The Indian team carried their star bowler to the pavilion, while the 25,000 fans danced and chanted his name, some of them running on to grab his shirt, which got torn in the pandemonium. Outside the ground a snake-charmer played his pipe. An Indian newspaper commemorated the event with the headline 'AK-74', referring to the number of runs Kumble had conceded in taking the ten wickets. The man himself commented: 'I would like to take this wicket with me wherever I go.'

India's next match was in the Asian Test Championship the following week, where their opponents were again Pakistan. At a function before the match Javagal Srinath made an appeal to his team-mate: 'Please remember, Anil, that there are other bowlers in the team too. You can't keep taking ten wickets all the time.' As if to follow through on this, Srinath then took eight wickets in Pakistan's second innings, Kumble bagging only a single batsman in the whole match. But to this day no one has repeated the feat of dismissing an entire Test side.

1878: second Wimbledon tennis championship

'A sissy's game played with a soft ball' – the verdict on tennis of the second man to win its most prestigious title.

Frank Hadow was the owner of a coffee plantation in Ceylon, who had only entered the second Men's Singles competition at Wimbledon after being persuaded by his friend Robert Erskine (whose real first name was Lestocq). Like six of his seven brothers, Frank had attended Harrow

School – they were known as the Harrow Hadows – but now tended his coffee beans in the imperial outpost, and was only in London on a visit. He, Erskine and 32 other men competed for the right to challenge Spencer Gore, the inaugural champion from 1877 who under the rules of the time received a bye through to the final. The gentlemen's was the only final that year – it would be 1884 before the ladies got a competition.

Professionals were banned from playing back then, so the courts at the All England club on Wimbledon's Nursery Road (they have since moved) were graced only by amateurs. As well as Hadow and Erskine there were the Montgomerie brothers George and Seton: the former would succeed their father as Earl of Eglinton, while the latter's wife Viva was the author of *Sunny Days on the Riviera, Being a Diary of Some Sketching at Èze*. Also taking part was Arthur Myers, the first player to serve overhand, as well as Herbert Lawford, the man who introduced top-spin to the game.

Hadow defeated Erskine to win the 'All Comers' final, so giving him the right to challenge Gore. The match took place on 18 July in front of 700 spectators. Hadow won 7–5, 6–1, 9–7, partly due to his innovative tactic of lobbing the ball, which helped nullify Gore's volleying game. Though Hadow had slightly less space to lob into than he would have done the previous year – the distance from service line to net was reduced by 4 feet to 22 feet. The height of the net was also reduced, by 3 inches to exactly 3 feet.

Asked if he would defend his title, Hadow said: 'No, sir. It's a sissy's game played with a soft ball.' So he remains the only Wimbledon singles champion never to have lost a set in the championship. He concentrated instead on his beloved big-game hunting in Africa, bagging records in the categories of sable antelope, Cape buffalo and Uganda kob.

Henri Cornet: second winner of the Tour de France

The Tour de France has had its brushes with scandal in recent years. Surely these are the result of the huge amounts of money in modern cycling? The early years of the race must have been a very different time, with sportsmanship and honesty the order of the day? Think again.

The Tour's very existence was down to money: the organiser, Henri Desgrange, only started it to promote his daily sports newspaper *L'Auto*. The inaugural race in 1903 was a great success, so the following year defending champion Maurice Garin and several dozen other riders gathered to repeat the event. One of them, Henri Paret, was 50 – still the oldest competitor ever to take part. To attract attention to the race Desgrange gave his riders nicknames. Henri Cornet, a talented 19-year-old, was 'Le rigolo' ('the joker') because of his sense of fun.

He'd need it over the next 1,509 miles. Fans of particular riders tried to jeopardise their rivals' chances by cutting down trees to block their path, spreading nails on the road to give them punctures and – taking as direct an approach as possible – beating them up. Near St Étienne supporters of local boy Antoine Fauré attacked the Italian rider Giovanni Gerbi. 'He is thrown to the ground,' ran one account, 'beaten like plaster. He escapes with a broken finger.' Maurice Garin was hit in the face with a stone, but remained confident: 'I'll win the Tour de France provided I'm not murdered before we get to Paris.' During the penultimate stage Henri Cornet fell victim to nails on the road. As mechanical assistance was forbidden he had to ride the last 25 miles on two flat tyres.

Not that the riders were whiter than white themselves. Garin was given food (against the rules) by race director Géo Lefèvre. Competitors had themselves towed along by cars, or simply got into the car for a lift. Others took the train. Nine of them were disqualified during the race, and although the race organisers declared themselves happy with the result – Garin had again come out on top – complaints about widespread cheating forced them to hold an inquiry. Eventually the first four finishers (including someone named Hippolyte Aucouturier) were eliminated, leaving fifth-placed Henri Cornet – who had come in three hours behind Garin – as the winner. It wasn't exactly a case of the good guy triumphing in the end: Cornet himself received an official warning for travelling part of the race in a car.

The full findings of the inquiry will never be known: the Tour's archives disappeared when they were moved in 1940 to protect them from the German invasion. But what we can say for sure is that Cornet remains, at a few days short of his 20th birthday, the race's youngest-ever winner.

1836: second Boat Race

Seven years and 30-odd miles separate this second from its first. The inaugural Boat Race in 1829 had taken place at Henley-on-Thames, the result of a challenge between friends Charles Wordsworth and Charles Merivale, who had attended Harrow School together but were then studying at Oxford and Cambridge Universities respectively. Wordsworth's comment in the run-up to the race that 'matters are proceeding swimmingly' might have been worded more carefully, but his confidence was well placed: Oxford won easily.

There was no attempt at a rematch until 1834, and even then it took a further two years for disagreements to be ironed out. Cambridge wanted to race on the Thames in London, while Oxford preferred Maidenhead. Eventually they agreed to race in the capital, but the final distance was only decided at a meeting in the Star and Garter pub in Putney the night before the race. Oxford wanted a short race of 1.5 miles, but had to settle for the 5.75 miles between Westminster Bridge and Putney Bridge.

The following day, 17 June, saw the heavens open in the afternoon, but according to the *Morning Post*, 'although the rain descended in torrents, all were gay'. Lots of people had turned up to watch. 'Long before the time appointed for the match,' ran one report, 'there was not a cutter to be obtained at any of the boat-builders' premises.'

Both teams sported some fine names. Oxford's crew included Justinian Vere Isham, John Pennefather and Frederick Lutterell Moysey, while Cambridge had Perceval Hartley, Arthur Wilson Upcher and Augustus Ker Bozzi Granville. Oxford were the favourites, and not simply because they'd supplied both the umpires. But when the race started at 4.20 p.m., Cambridge pulled clear. By Vauxhall Bridge their lead was significant, one observer noting that they were rowing 'gallantly'. The result was never in doubt: they finished the race in a time of 36 minutes, a minute and 20 lengths ahead of Oxford. They had levelled the series at 1–1.

The Sportsman magazine was unimpressed with the rowers' technique. 'It was surprising,' it wrote of one Oxford crew member, 'that he did not shake his head off his shoulders by his frequent bobbings.' But we must remember that conditions were much harder in those days. The sliding seat had not yet been invented, though the crew did sometimes grease the backsides of their trousers.

There were more irregular races after this, but it would be 1856 before the Boat Race became an annual event. The second race was notable for being the debut of the 'dark blue/light blue' tradition. Oxford had worn dark blue in the first event (because four of their crew were from Christ Church, whose college colours were dark blue). They repeated this in 1836 – and Cambridge wore light blue, possibly because this is the colour of Eton, where several of their crew had studied.

Peter Norman: second place in the 1968 200-metre Olympic final

The medallists' podium for the men's 200-metre final at the 1968 Olympics in Mexico City produced one of the most famous images in all of sport: the black American athletes John Carlos and Tommie Smith raising their fists in the 'Black Power' salute while their nation's anthem was played. But there was another man on the podium – the silver medallist, white Australian runner Peter Norman. His support for Carlos and Smith would end up costing him his career.

Born to Salvation Army parents in Melbourne, Norman couldn't afford the kit to play his favourite sport of Australian

Rules football. But his father borrowed a pair of running shoes for his son, and young Peter's talent was soon apparent. As he grew up he refused to obey the Salvation Army's teaching about not running on a Sunday, but still had the words 'God is Love' stitched on the back of his tracksuit.

Arriving in Mexico for the 1968 Olympics, Norman was delighted to find that the thin air at that altitude allowed his stride to lengthen: 'I could feel my knees bouncing around my chin.' He won his 200-metre heat with a time of 20.17 seconds, which briefly stood as the Olympic record. In the final he knew that Tommie Smith was unbeatable – 'you wouldn't be able to catch him on a motorbike' – but surprised everyone by overtaking Carlos to claim second place.

The Americans told the Australian what they were planning to do during the medal ceremony. Carlos expected to see fear in Norman's eyes, but instead 'I saw love'. Norman replied: 'I'll stand with you.' (Norman had previously criticised Australia's own policy of restricting non-white immigration and oppressing its aboriginal people.) On their way out to the podium he saw a member of the US rowing team wearing an 'Olympic Project for Human Rights' badge, and asked if he could borrow it. He pinned it to his left breast. Carlos and Smith had both removed their shoes to symbolise black poverty. Carlos wore a black scarf to denote black pride, and Smith left his tracksuit top unzipped to signal solidarity with blue-collar workers. The final sartorial touch – each runner wearing a single glove – was Norman's idea. The sprinters had meant to wear a pair of gloves each, but when Carlos accidentally left his at the Olympic Village, Norman suggested they simply share Smith's pair. Carlos wore the left glove, Smith the right.

The medals were presented by former athlete David Burghley (who as a young man had become the first to run all the way round Great Court at Magdalene College, Cambridge, within the time it took the college clock to strike twelve – the inspiration for the famous scene in *Chariots of Fire*). Norman was on the left, Smith in the middle and Carlos on the right, meaning that when they all turned to their right to face the flags, the other two were behind Norman. 'I couldn't see what was happening,' he said later, but he knew 'they had gone through with their plans when a voice in the crowd sang the American anthem but then faded to nothing. The stadium went quiet.'

As did Norman's own career. Back in Australia he was shunned, and despite running the necessary qualifying times he was left out of the 1972 Olympics in Munich. He retired from competitive running, but didn't hang up his trainers for good until 1985, when an injury became infected and he contracted gangrene. It was thought amputation would be necessary, but a doctor argued that 'you can't cut the leg off an Olympic silver medallist'. In hospital Norman used his silver medal as a doorstop.

The stigma continued all the way to 2000, when Sydney hosted the games and Norman was the only Australian Olympian not invited to do a lap of honour. This despite the fact his 1968 time of 20.06 seconds would have won the 200 metres that year, and indeed still stands as the Australian record to this day. However, the US team flew him to Sydney, where that year's 200-metre champion Michael Johnson hugged him and said: 'You are my hero.'

Eventually, in 2012, Norman received an apology from the Australian government for his treatment. This would have been nicer for him had he not died in 2006. John Carlos and Tommie Smith flew to Australia to be pallbearers at his funeral. 'If we were getting beat up,' Carlos said, 'Peter was facing an entire country and suffering alone.'

A 23-foot statue of the two black runners stands at San José State University, their fists raised as they were on the podium. The silver medallist's spot is empty – it's where tourists stand to have their picture taken. But Tommie Smith knows the truth about Peter Norman: 'While he didn't raise a fist, he did lend a hand.'

Ronnie Ray Smith: second person to run 100 metres in under ten seconds

This must be the smallest gap ever between a first and its second – in fact according to the clocks used on the night there was no gap at all. No athlete had ever run a legal (that is, non-wind-assisted) time of under ten seconds for the 100 metres, but on 20 June 1968, in the first semi-final of the USA Outdoor Track and Field Championships, Jim Hines did just that. As did the man in second place, 19-year-old Ronnie Ray Smith. And because the timings in those days were done by hand, and only rounded to one decimal place, both men were marked at 9.9 seconds. The same time would be achieved by Charles Greene, winner of the second semi-final, earning that evening at the Hughes Stadium in Sacramento, California, the title 'the Night of Speed'.

Later that year Smith would achieve fame at the Olympics as the runner of the third leg in the American 4 x 100-metre relay team. Their winning time of 38.24 seconds was a new world record. Hines and Greene were also members of the quartet. These were the same games at which Tommie Smith and John Carlos performed their famous 'Black Power' salute (see 'Peter Norman', p. 103). Smith was one of four graduates of San José State College to win gold medals in track and field events at the games, making the institution's haul greater than that of every country except America.

Smith died in 2013. His funeral featured in a TV series called *Best Funeral Ever*, and involved his coffin being displayed vertically on an Olympic-style podium before its burial.

1900: second modern Olympic Games

Paris had wanted to host the first modern Olympics in 1896, but that honour was awarded to Athens. However, the French capital secured one first – unlike at the previous games, women were allowed to compete. Hélène de Pourtalès became the first female Olympic champion, as part of the Swiss team which crewed the boat *Lérina* to victory in the 2–3-ton class. The British competitor Charlotte Cooper gained the first individual gold medal by winning the women's tennis singles.

The games had several moments of controversy. The American Alvin Kraenzlein received a punch in the face for his victory in the long jump: his rival Myer Prinstein was unhappy at Kranzlein breaking their agreement not to compete in the final because it was being held on a Sunday. (Many of the US athletes had taken this approach.) The marathon was particularly contentious. The course, which wound through the streets of Paris, was poorly marked, and several competitors got lost, having to retrace their steps before continuing. Two American runners contested the result. Arthur Newton finished fifth but maintained he hadn't been passed by anyone, while Richard Grant claimed a cyclist had run him down as he was gaining on the leaders. French runners were awarded first and second places, but the Americans said they must have taken a short cut: they were the only runners whose shirts weren't splattered with mud.

The games were the only ones in Olympic history to use live pigeons as targets in the shooting competition. Other unusual events included the swimming obstacle race, in which competitors had to both swim underneath and climb over rows of boats, and the underwater swimming race, won by Charles Devendeville, who stayed submerged for over a minute. The water-polo winners were the Osborne Swimming Club of Manchester, whose three matches saw them score 29 goals and concede only three. In the final they deliberately went easy on their opponents to avoid humiliating them.

The croquet tournament attracted just a single paying spectator, an elderly English gentleman who had travelled from Nice to watch. The competitors in the cricket match (only two teams took part) didn't even know they were competing in the Olympics – they thought they were participating in the World's Fair that was taking place in Paris at the same time. The French side was made up mostly of British expats, while the British team was the Devon and Somerset Wanderers, only two of whom were good enough to have played for Somerset. If the French had managed to bat for five minutes longer they would have secured a draw, but Britain bagged the victory. It was only in 1912 that the players were informed that the International Olympic Committee had given their match Olympic status, adding gold (Britain) and silver (France) medals to the miniature Eiffel Towers awarded at the time. Because cricket has never featured in the Games since, Britain are the reigning Olympic champions.

Trevor Wright: second-fastest time in the first London marathon

In terms of placings, Trevor Wright is a third. In terms of timings, he's a second. That's because in 1981, towards the end of the inaugural London marathon, the two leading runners decided to cross the finish line together. Dick Beardsley of the USA and the Norwegian Inge Simonsen felt it would be in the spirit of the event to finish as joint winners, so they held hands and recorded identical times of two hours, 11 minutes and 48 seconds. Beardsley – the only man ever to run 13 consecutive personal bests in the marathon – said later: 'It was a big deal for both of us because neither one of us had won a marathon before.' Britain's Trevor Wright crossed the line one minute and five seconds later. He was into the second decade of his marathon career, having set the world record for fastest debut marathon in 1971. An electrician at a waterworks in Wednesbury, he trained by running the several miles home from work every day. He continued this practice after emigrating to New Zealand in 1982, though his run through the countryside there was rather more scenic than his route in the West Midlands.

Wright's wife Rosemary was also a runner, finishing 16th in the women's race that day in 1981. The oldest competitor was 78-year-old Bob Wiseman, who finished in 'six hours plus' – the official clock had stopped by the time he crossed the finish line. He'd been waved off at the start by family members including seven great-grandchildren.

The second London marathon (1982) was won by Britain's Hugh Jones. He can't recall sleeping at all the night before the event, but didn't panic: the same thing had happened a few months previously before the Tokyo marathon, and his coach had told him it didn't matter – as long as he rested and avoided worrying, all would be well. The same wasn't true at the 1995 Barbados marathon, when 250 yards from the end, leading by three minutes, Jones collapsed from heatstroke. But he didn't know it was heatstroke – he simply thought he had fallen. When his attempts to get up failed he started crawling to the finish line. When he couldn't crawl, he started to roll. At this point some worried marshals came to his aid, putting him on a drip and carrying him to hospital. He forfeited the race.

Jones now measures distances for marathon courses, including both the London marathon itself (which is constantly being tweaked) and the city's course for the 2012 Olympics. He works on a bicycle, not trusting GPS. 'It's hopeless, absolutely hopeless. It's pretty good if you're in the North Pole or the Sahara Desert, but if you're in Canary Wharf the signals go completely haywire.'

Roger Maris: second US baseball player to hit 60 home runs in a season

The most famous baseball player ever is Babe Ruth. One of his many achievements was becoming, in 1927, the first player ever to hit 60 home runs in a season. So exceptional was this total that many fans thought it would never be repeated. But someone finally *did* manage it – and received so much criticism for even daring to match Babe Ruth that the stress made his hair fall out.

Like Ruth, Roger Maris and Mickey Mantle played for the New York Yankees. They were known as the M&M boys (after the chocolates that had been around since 1941). In 1961 they engaged in a duel to be the first to match Ruth's 60 runs in a season. It was a contest that would be marked by drama, injury and off-the-field politics.

Mantle already knew how protective Yankees fans were of their hero's record. In 1956, when it looked as though he might score 60 home runs, there were noises of disquiet. He finally finished the season on 52, much to the relief of many. In his early career Mantle had antagonised the New York press, being seen as a hick from Oklahoma. But over the years he had learned to cultivate the media. It was a further example of his capacity for knuckling down: during a slump in form during his first season (1951), when he played for the Kansas City Blues, he had called his father to say he couldn't carry on. His father drove up to see him, started packing his son's clothes and said: 'I thought I raised a man. I see I raised a coward instead. You can come back to Oklahoma and work the mines with me.' Mantle stayed, improved his form and earned a transfer to the Yankees, where he once came close to becoming the only player ever to hit the ball out of the stadium during a game. By 1961 he was the highest-paid player in the whole league, earning $75,000. Two years later he would reach $100,000, and never asked for another raise. The highest-paid player in 2017 was Clayton Kershaw of the LA Dodgers, who earned $33m.

That season the schedule was extended from 154 games to 162. Asked if this might help a player beat Ruth's record, Maris replied: 'Nobody will touch it . . . Look up the records and you'll see that it's a rare year when anybody hits fifty homers, let alone sixty.' But by June it was clear that not just Maris himself but also Mantle had a chance of breaking Ruth's record. The press tried to paint them as bitter rivals, but they actually remained good friends, sharing an apartment in Queens. Mantle tried to pass on the advice he'd received about keeping the media onside, but Maris maintained his plain-speaking ways, and continued to be seen by both press and fans as an unsympathetic figure. Everyone wanted Mantle to win the race. The lead changed hands between the two players several times as the season progressed.

On 17 July, however, Ford Frick, the Commissioner of Baseball (the game's chief executive) ruled that for a new record to count it would have to be achieved within 154 games – the number Babe Ruth had played – rather than the full 162. If not, it would be shown in the record books as having taken longer, and Ruth's record would still be included. The fact that Frick was a close personal friend of Ruth may or may not have influenced his decision. On 15 August Maris passed Mantle once more, and as they entered September was on 56 home runs to Mantle's 53. But then disaster struck for Mantle: an anti-flu injection had caused an abscess in his hip joint, which now rendered him incapable of playing. Despite the so-called 'rift' he cheered Maris on from his hospital bed.

This was more than most Yankees fans were doing. Maris remained unpopular. The stress of chasing the total was so great that clumps of his hair sometimes fell out. 'I'm not trying to be Babe Ruth,' he protested. 'I'm trying to hit sixty-one home runs and be Roger Maris.' His protestations had no effect. 'They acted as though I was doing something wrong,' he said years later, 'poisoning the record books or something. Do you know what I have to show for 61 home runs? Nothing. Exactly nothing.' He even expressed the thought that it might have been better had he not broken the record at all.

After 154 games Maris had 59 home runs, so failed the criterion set by Frick. But when he did reach 60 it was in fewer plate appearances (turns at batting) than Babe Ruth had managed (684 to 689). He was still on 60 when the final game of the season came round on 1 October. Only 23,154 people turned up at Yankee Stadium, a sign of the lack of support for the man who could still break Ruth's record. And break it he did, hitting his 61st home run. Sal Durante, the fan who caught the ball, offered to return it to Maris. The player declined, telling Durante to sell it and make some money for himself. A restaurant owner paid $5,000 for the ball, then promptly gave it to Maris. Several years later Maris donated it to the National Baseball Hall of Fame and Museum.

Maris and Mantle went on to launch a clothing business together. Maris also operated the Budweiser distributorship in Gainesville, Florida, after his retirement. The Yankees retired his number nine shirt (as they had retired Mantle's number seven). Maris died of non-Hodgkin lymphoma in 1985 at the age of 51. In 1999 the US Postal Service issued a 'Roger Maris, 61 in 61' stamp as part of their 'Celebrate the Century' series. But to this day the player has still not been elected to baseball's Hall of Fame. By common consent this is because of his awkward relations with the media, some of whom have votes in the process. Maris himself once said: 'I'll leave the Hall of Fame to the geniuses that vote on it. I will never get in. I have always known that.'

NATURE

◆

K2: second-highest mountain in the world

K2 might not be as high as Mount Everest (28,251 feet plays 29,029), but it's certainly more difficult to climb. Its nickname 'the Savage Mountain' is testament to the opinion held by many climbers: K2 is the most dangerous mountain in the world. Only around 300 people have reached the summit (compared to nearly 3,000 for Everest), and having caused 77 deaths it has one of the highest fatality ratios of any mountain. In fact K2 comes second in that list too: among the world's mountains over 8,000 feet, only Annapurna I (also in the Himalayas) is more deadly. But Annapurna I has been climbed in winter – to this day no one has managed that feat on K2.

You'd expect nothing less from a mountain whose features include the Black Pyramid, the Hockey Stick, the Eagle's Nest, House's Chimney and the Bottleneck. But despite these dramatic names, the mountain as a whole retains its rather anonymous title. 'K2' was one of the two most prominent peaks in the Karakoram range mapped by Thomas Montgomerie during the Great Trigonometric Survey of the 19th century. K1 soon became known by its local name,

Masherbrum, but the other peak was so remote it didn't even *have* a local name: it was invisible from Askole, the nearest village.

The name Mount Godwin-Austen was suggested, after Henry Godwin-Austen who had explored the area. In the same way, 'Peak XV' was named after one-time leader of the Great Trigonometric Survey George Everest – who actually pronounced it 'Eev-rest'. The taller mountain's new title stuck, but K2 – perhaps fittingly, given its 'second' status – remained K2. The Italian mountaineer Fosco Maraini thought the name apt for a different reason. It reflected the mountain's character, he said: 'Just the bare bones of a name, all rock and ice and storm and abyss. It makes no attempt to sound human.'

The first attempt on the summit was in 1902, by a party including the legendary occultist Aleister Crowley, once dubbed 'the wickedest man in the world'. He was a serious mountaineer: having started by climbing Beachy Head, he had progressed to several of the most difficult peaks in the Alps. But on the K2 climb he suffered flu, snow blindness and malaria. The attempt failed. Seven years later the Italian Prince Luigi Amedeo, Duke of the Abruzzi, reached 20,510 feet, but could climb no higher. The mountain's uniformly steep shape led him to declare that it would never be conquered.

It took another 46 years, but the Duke was eventually proved wrong. The 1954 expedition led by his compatriot Ardito Desio reached the summit on 31 July. A Pakistani porter, Amir Mehdi, carried oxygen tanks to 26,600 feet, allowing Desio and two others to complete the climb. Mehdi had to have his toes amputated because of frostbite. It would be a further 23 years before a second expedition conquered the mountain. On 9 August 1977 the Japanese climber Ichiro Yoshizawa reached the summit, along with Ashraf Aman of Pakistan. Yoshizawa was an incredibly courteous man – in the 1960s, when an American colleague's plane touched down at 3 a.m. to refuel at Tokyo airport, he drove an hour each way through a storm to spend 15 minutes with him in the transit lounge.

Arabian Desert: second-largest desert in the world

The 899,618 square miles of the Arabian Desert were once joined to the 3,552,140 square miles of the Sahara Desert. Then, 5 million years ago or so, a movement in the Earth's crust separated Arabia from Africa. Appropriately, given the fact the two areas were once joined, the Sahara takes its name from the Arabic word for 'desert'. Even older movements of the Earth's plates had allowed a substance to form between the layers of rock that are today the most important thing in the Arabian Desert: oil.

The desert stretches from Yemen in the south to Iraq in the north, from the Red Sea in the west to the Persian Gulf in the east. It contains every sort of terrain, from red dunes to quicksand. In the region known as the Rub' al Khali (Arabic for 'Empty Quarter') lies the Umm al Samim, an area of quicksand formed of salt marsh covered in a crust that looks solid but can be broken through. So treacherous is the area that its local nickname is 'Mother of Worries'.

Summer temperatures in the subtropical climate can reach 55 degrees Celsius, but there is life: the raq shrub, for example, known as the 'toothbrush' bush, because that's what its twigs are traditionally used for. The Dhofar region of Oman also contains the shrubs that yield two of the most famous substances in history: frankincense and myrrh. Insect life includes the mantids, which camouflage themselves as leaves or pebbles, while the dab is a 3-foot-long lizard, vegetarian and toothless, whose fat tail, when roasted, is a Bedouin delicacy.

The most famous occurrence of the word 'desert' in recent years was when the Americans added the word 'Operation' before it and 'Storm' after it. During the 1991 Gulf War their tanks disrupted the desert's top layer of soil to such an extent that a huge sand dune was released. This started moving slowly downhill, with some people suggesting that it could eventually reach Kuwait City. 'Desert Storm', incidentally, was only the codename for the US operations. Britain's efforts in the war were Operation Granby, named after John Manners, the Marquess of Granby, who served as a British commander during the Seven Years War of the 18th century. He was known for treating his troops well and being held in high regard by them. Indeed the Marquess is said to be the person who has more pubs named after him than anyone else: he often set up members of his regiment as landlords when they were no longer young enough to fight.

Cherrapunji: second-wettest place on Earth

Think the Lake District is wet? Try Meghalaya in India. The area where Wordsworth admired the daffodils gets about 2,000mm of rainfall per year – Meghalaya gets over 11,000mm. The very highest figure is achieved at Mawsynram (11,873mm). The second-wettest place on Earth, with 11,430mm, is Cherrapunji. Most of the rain falls during the monsoon season of June to September. At other times of year the area can actually suffer droughts. A further irony is that despite their copious drenching each year, many local people have to travel long distances to obtain water they can drink.

The rainfall at Cherrapunji is 'orographic precipitation' – in other words it's caused by air getting forced rapidly upwards as it meets steep terrain (in this case the Khasi Hills), thereby producing clouds which then deposit rain. It's the same process – albeit on a much greater scale – that produces rain near the Pennines. However, people in the north of England don't have to resort to 'knups', the rain shields that residents of Cherrapunji weave from reeds and wear over their heads and backs. Unlike an umbrella, the knup leaves both your hands free for working.

Conventional building materials would rot away in such wet conditions, so bridges in the area are made by guiding the roots of rubber fig trees across any gap that needs to be crossed. This is sometimes achieved with the aid of bamboo scaffolding. When the roots grow strong they become a 'living' bridge that can support the weight of a human.

The Sanskrit meaning of Meghalaya is 'land of the clouds'. During the days of the British Raj, however, the state's climate led to it being nicknamed 'the Scotland of the East'.

Tonga Trench: second-deepest part of the ocean

Were you to place Mount Everest in the Tonga Trench, there would still be room between its peak and the surface of the water for you to add Ben Nevis, with the Shard balanced on top of it – and another Shard balanced on top of that. The Tonga's maximum depth of 35,433 feet (the part known as the Horizon Deep) is beaten only by the Challenger Deep in the Mariana Trench (36,069 feet). Both are in the Pacific Ocean – the Tonga between New Zealand and Tonga itself, the Mariana to the east of the Philippines.

The first ship to discover seriously deep water in the vicinity was HMS *Egeria*, an 1880s British vessel named after a water nymph from Roman mythology. The Horizon Deep is named after the research vessel *Horizon*, which discovered it in December 1952. Plates at the edge of the Tonga have recently been measured as moving at 9.4 inches per year, making them the fastest plates on Earth.

For a long time scientists didn't believe that life was possible at such depths: there is almost no light, the oxygen is literally centuries old (it takes that long to filter down), and the pressure is a ton per square centimetre – the equivalent of 1,600 elephants standing on the roof of a Mini. But modern research has established that, against all the odds, creatures do inhabit the trench. There are nematode worms, the basic beings so small that their density can exceed one million per square metre, and which account for 80 per cent of all the individual animals on Earth. And in 2007, a craft sent to survey the trench found rat-tail fish and snail fish, the latter a pink, slimy creature with tiny black eyes and an orange blob that on closer examination proved to be its internal organs. The brown-snout spookfish has also been found in the Tonga. Each of its eyes is divided into two, one section looking up, the other down, giving it the appearance of having four eyes. Scientists were also amazed to find that the spookfish focuses light onto its retinas via stacked plates of guanine (a protein). In such dark conditions, once you've found a mate you don't want to lose it, so when the male angler fish bumps into a female he latches onto her with his lips and never lets go. One biologist has described this as 'a kiss that lasts the rest of his life'. From then on the fish doesn't feed – instead he 'hooks up to her blood supply'.

But the biggest snap in the Tonga Trench is a SNAP – the Systems Nuclear Auxiliary Power unit from Apollo 13. Each lunar craft carried one of these tanks containing radioactive fuel. Most were left on the surface of the Moon, but because Apollo 13's mission was aborted its tank fell into the trench. Monitoring of the ocean has indicated no release of nuclear material.

The Danube: second-longest river in Europe

The Danube's journey from Germany to the Black Sea lasts 1,780 miles, making it 514 miles shorter than the Volga. But that trip takes it through ten countries – more than any other river in the world – and four national capitals, also a world record. They are Vienna (Austria), Bratislava (Slovakia), Budapest (Hungary) and Belgrade (Serbia). Indeed the Danube is referred to in the Austrian national anthem, which begins, 'Land of mountains, land by the river'. It also gets a nod in Bulgaria's anthem: 'Proud old Balkan mountains, shining near the Danube'.

Fittingly for such a well-travelled river, the Danube is classified as an international waterway so that Austria, Hungary, Moldova, Serbia and Slovakia – all landlocked countries – can have access to the Black Sea. In Slovakia there is an island (Žitný ostrov) between the Danube and two of its tributaries – at 728 square miles it is the largest river island in Europe.

An article in *The Times* of 13 February 1883 said the Danube was 'annually swept by ice that will lift a large ship out of the water or cut her in two as if she were a carrot'. But the river's name elicits gentler reactions in modern souls, probably because of the soothing tones of 'The Blue Danube', Johann Strauss's ode to the waterway of his native Vienna. 'Blue Danube' was the codename for Britain's first operational nuclear weapon, and also the name of the band that represented Austria in the 1980 Eurovision Song Contest – they came eighth out of 19 with 'Du bist Musik' ('You Are Music'). But the waltz itself is best known these days for its inclusion in the soundtrack to Stanley Kubrick's film *2001: A Space Odyssey*. Like the other classical pieces in the movie, 'The Blue Danube' was originally intended merely as a guide for Kubrick to edit to while composer Alex North wrote the film's actual score. But the director liked the result so much that he left the pieces in place. North only discovered this when he saw the film at its premiere.

New Guinea: second-largest island in the world

'Island' is one of those words whose precise definition be-
comes less clear the more you think about it – after all, any
land mass surrounded by sea could be termed an island. But
by common consent Australia is a continent (the world's
smallest), making Greenland the world's largest island.
Runner-up – 303,381 square miles to Greenland's 822,700
– is New Guinea.

The island got its modern name when 16th-century Spanish explorers arrived and noted that the indigenous tribes
looked similar to the people they had encountered in the
Guinea region of Africa. These days the eastern part of the
island is Papua New Guinea, an independent country since
1975, while the western part is administered by Indonesia,
and is split into two provinces, West Papua and Papua. The
island's shape is similar to that of a bird of paradise found
there, so the north-west and south-east tips are known as
Bird's Head Peninsula and Bird's Tail Peninsula respectively.

New Guinea is a naturalist's dream. In the ten years
from 1998 over 1,000 previously undiscovered species of
mammals, fish and birds were identified there. The island
takes up less than 0.5 per cent of the Earth's surface, yet
contains between 5 and 10 per cent of its species. It is also
the most linguistically diverse place on the planet, with over
1,000 languages having been identified. This isn't surprising
for somewhere with so many tribes: a 2013 estimate put the
number of uncontacted tribes in the world at about 100,
over a third of which are thought to be on New Guinea.

The main language is Tok Pisin, a Creole language
sometimes known as New Guinea Pidgin. The English

derivation of many of its words gives rise to some wonderful expressions. 'Woman', for instance, is *meri* (from the name 'Mary'), while 'elbow' is *skru bilong han* ('the screw that belongs in the arm'). 'Hair' is *gras bilong het* ('head grass'), and 'moustache' is *aus gras* ('mouth grass'). 'Toothpaste' is *sop bilong tit* ('teeth soap'). 'Helicopter' is *magimiks bilong Yesus* ('Jesus's Magimix').

If you're angry you are *belhat* ('belly hot'). This could be because something is *bagarap* ('broken', derived from 'bugger up'). When Prince Charles visited New Guinea in 2012 he introduced himself as the *nambawan pikinini bilong misis kwin* – 'number one child belonging to Mrs Queen'.

Sequoia National Park: second-oldest national park in the US

Named after the variety of tree that covers much of its 404,064 acres, Sequoia became a national park in 1890. Five of the world's ten largest trees are to be found in its Californian vastness, including the biggest of them all, the giant sequoia known as General Sherman, whose volume is 52,508 cubic feet. The world's second-largest tree, the General Grant in Kings Canyon National Park, was declared a national shrine – a memorial to all those who died in war – by President Eisenhower in 1956. It's the only living object to achieve this status. The General Grant is believed to be about 1,650 years old. 'Tunnel Log', meanwhile, is another giant sequoia. It fell across one of the park's roads in 1937 and has been there ever since, an 8-foot-tall hole cut in its trunk to allow cars to drive through.

Sequoia also contains the highest mountain in the 'Lower

48' (the name used to denote the US states excluding Hawaii and Alaska). This is the 14,505-foot Mount Whitney, named after Josiah Whitney, a geologist who didn't always get on too well with the officials who funded his surveys. 'We have escaped perils by flood and field,' he once wrote, 'have evaded the friendly embrace of the grizzly, and now find ourselves in the jaws of the Legislature.' (The park's black bears sometimes break into unattended cars to steal food.) In 1873 one of Whitney's contemporaries, Clarence King, became the second person to climb Mount Whitney. He'd thought he was the first, but discovered that the peak he'd ascended two years earlier was actually Mount Langley. As a geologist, being known as the man who got a mountain wrong can't have been easy. King then climbed the real Mount Whitney, but not before someone else had got there first.

In 2016 a child's letter to the park authorities proved a big hit on social media: 'To whom it may concern, I took a pine cone out of the forest and I wanted to return it. I hope it will be placed near the General Grant tree because that is where I took it. I am sorry for my decision. Thank you.'

The first US national park, Yellowstone (granted its status by President Ulysses S. Grant in 1872), was the inspiration for Jellystone, the park frequented by Yogi Bear. The second man to provide the cartoon character's voice was Greg Burson, who replaced Daws Butler after the latter's death in 1988. The following year saw the death of Mel Blanc, the voice of Bugs Bunny, and Burson replaced him too. Sadly Burson's career came to an end in 2004 after an incident in which he barricaded himself inside his home with a hostage. 'He was so drunk,' said one of the police officers who attended, 'we couldn't tell if he was trying to do one of his voices or was just slurring his words.'

Lake Tanganyika: second-largest freshwater lake in the world

This majestic corner of Africa doesn't just come second in the 'largest-by-volume' stakes. It is also the world's second-deepest freshwater lake, as well as the second-oldest. First place in all these categories is held by Russia's Lake Baikal. And water from Tanganyika flows (via the Lukuga River) into the Congo, the second-longest river in Africa. But Tanganyika does get one gold medal: it is the longest freshwater lake on the planet.

You could get your head round its size by learning that it holds 16 per cent of the world's available supply of fresh water (4,534 cubic miles of the stuff). Or that it has its own endemic wildlife, including types of sardines, sprats and jellyfish found nowhere else. But perhaps the best indicator of Lake Tanganyika's hugeness is that it has shores in four countries: Zambia, Burundi, Democratic Republic of the Congo and Tanzania. The latter's name came about with the merger of Tanganyika (the country) and Zanzibar, who combined their first syllables.

The first Westerners to see the lake were the British explorers Richard Burton and John Speke in 1858, as they searched for the source of the Nile. In fact, Speke saw it second – he was initially unable to view the lake, having been temporarily blinded by a tropical disease. Many more Westerners visited during World War I, when the British and German navies fought the Battle for Lake Tanganyika. This conflict, which inspired the novel and film *The African Queen*, was eventually won by the British. During the German retreat the captain of the vessel *Graf von Goetzen* ordered it to be scuttled. Before the war this ferry had been built in Germany, disassembled and packed into 5,000 crates, loaded onto three cargo ships and taken to Africa, where it had been reassembled. In 1924 the British raised it from the lake and found that it had been so well preserved by greasing that very little work was necessary to return it to service. This happened in 1927. Now under the name *Liemba*, the ship still operates as a passenger ferry – the last vessel of the German Imperial Navy still sailing anywhere in the world.

Bud Rogan: second-tallest man ever

Until recently a lifesize model of the tallest man ever, Robert Pershing Wadlow (1918–40) stood outside the Ripley's Believe It or Not! attraction at London's Piccadilly Circus. His 8-foot-11-inch frame also earned him a mention on the 1980s BBC kids' TV show *Record Breakers*. The host, Roy Castle, sang a specially written song about him. No such fame for John 'Bud' Rogan, who was only 2 inches shorter than Wadlow.

Born in Tennessee in 1865, the son of a former black slave, Rogan was a normal child until the age of 13, when he succumbed to acromegaly, a condition in which the pituitary gland produces too much growth hormone. His maternal grandfather had also been abnormally tall, and needed an extra-large saddle for his horse. Bud soon passed the height of 8 feet: to this day he's one of fewer than 20 people to do so. Eventually his condition made it impossible for him to walk or even stand. Confined to his bed, he had materials brought to him from which he constructed a cart on which he could be pulled around by goats.

Using this transport he travelled every day from the home he shared with his mother (his father had by then died) to the train station in his town of Gallatin. Here he made a good living by selling postcards of himself to the passengers. The *Salt Lake Enquirer* wrote that he was 'of a happy disposition, courteous to all, and possessed a great deal of intelligence'. Famous as 'the Negro giant', Rogan refused all offers to join freak shows or travelling circuses. A few times he accepted invitations to travel to events like the World's Fair in Chicago, but he always backed out, afraid that he would 'be stolen'.

His hands were 11 inches long, his fingernails the size of 25-cent pieces. In 1899 the *Philadelphia Medical Journal* published an outline of his hand compared to that of a large man: the latter fitted entirely within Rogan's palm. (The journal had intended to print it actual size, but their pages were too small.) Rogan's feet were 13 inches long: he couldn't find shoes to fit them, so in cold weather had to wrap them in cloth. Similarly no hat was large enough for him. He made his own by putting two or three normal hats together.

Bud Rogan never stopped growing. His final height of 8 feet 9 inches wasn't measured until after his death, at the age of 37. His mother had him buried in her back yard, under a thick layer of concrete so that no one would steal his body.

Anna Bates: second-tallest woman ever

Until China's Zeng Jinlian (1964–82) reached her height of 8 feet 1 inch, the title of world's tallest-ever woman had belonged to Anna Bates, born in Nova Scotia in 1846. Her 12 siblings were all of average height, but it was clear from Anna's birth weight – 16 pounds – that she would be the exception. By the age of six she was 5 feet 2 inches, almost the same height as her mother. A couple of years later a passer-by stopped to see why a 'woman' was out playing with children. At school her desk had to be replaced by a table raised on planks, while at the family dinner table she sat on the floor with her back against the wall.

By the age of 15 Anna was 7 feet tall, and when she stopped growing three years later she measured 7 feet 11 inches. Her feet were 14 inches long. By then she had begun her career at P.T. Barnum's museum in New York, earning $23 per week in gold. She was often paired with Tom Thumb, who stood at 2 feet 5 inches. In 1865 the museum was destroyed in a fire. Trapped on an upper floor, Anna was too big to fit through the window. It was only when an outside wall was demolished and a crane brought in that she managed to escape.

In 1869, while touring America, Barnum and Anna met Martin Van Buren Bates, a Confederate captain from the Civil War who was just 4 inches shorter than Anna. The showman immediately hired him, and eventually the couple fell in love. They married at London's St Martin-in-the-Fields church in 1871, with a diamond ring provided by Queen Victoria. It must have been the only wedding at which the

6-foot-3-inch vicar felt small, and Mr and Mrs Bates remain the tallest married couple in history.

Having bought land in Ohio, Martin and Anna had a house built with 14-foot ceilings and 8-foot-6-inch doorways. (The back part of the house was built with normal dimensions, for their servants and guests.) Their furniture was also custom-built, providing relief after years of having to squeeze onto too-small chairs. Anna had once sat on one end of a friend's sofa, causing the other end to tip up in the air.

Anna bore two children by Bates, but neither of them lived more than a few hours. The second, a son born in 1879, weighed 23 pounds 9 ounces, making him to this day the largest human baby ever. Anna herself died unexpectedly the day before her 42nd birthday. Martin ordered a coffin from a company in Cleveland, but, assuming the dimensions were a mistake, they sent one of normal size. The replacement took a further three days to arrive.

Martin later remarried, but on his instructions he was buried with Anna and their two children. On top of her grave sits the statue of a Greek goddess he'd had placed there. It is 15 feet tall.

Tibia: second-longest bone in the human body

Averaging 16.9 inches, the tibia – your shin bone – is 3 inches shorter than your femur (thigh bone). But it is stronger: indeed it's the strongest bone in your body, as it has to bear almost all of your weight. The tibia is named after a Roman flute, whose shape it resembles. A more modern name for it – the shank – gave rise to the expression 'travelling by Shanks's pony' (walking). A goat's shank bone is one of the items of food on the Seder plate, served at the Jewish feast marking the beginning of Passover.

Sarah Knauss: second-oldest person ever

Longevity seems to be a woman's game. Of the longest-lived people ever (at the time of writing), the top 15 are female. In fact all but six of the top 100 are female. The record is held by France's Jeanne Calment, who died in 1997 at the age of 122 years, 164 days. She had already become a teenager when she met Vincent Van Gogh, but towards the end of her life had to stop making public appearances: it was explained that this 'allowed her to die, as the attention had kept her alive'. She also, at the age of 120, gave up smoking.

Second place belongs to Sarah Knauss, who lived for 119 years, 97 days. She was born Sarah DeRemer Clark on 24 September 1880, in Hollywood. Not that one – it didn't exist yet. This was Hollywood, Pennsylvania, a coal-mining village. Life expectancy back then was 40 years. Sarah would achieve nearly treble that.

In 1901 she married Abraham Knauss, whose middle name was Lincoln (this was only three decades after the President's assassination). The couple honeymooned at Niagara Falls, then set up home in Allentown, which was then still a small town. Sarah felt like an outsider because the grocery store assistants spoke in Pennsylvania Dutch. The town had horse-drawn trolleys – Sarah saw the last one ever finish its service.

In 1903 she gave birth to her only child, Kitty. In the 1920s the family got its first-ever refrigerator – before that, ice had been delivered by the ice man. For Christmas 1940, when she was already 60, Sarah received an electric sewing machine. She would make her own clothes and hem her family's clothes right up to her death – another 59 years. Her life was simple: watching TV (particularly golf and the QVC shopping channel), making pot pie and Moravian sugar cake, playing bridge with friends. She never flew in a plane or learned to drive. Kitty called her mother 'a happy warrior in her home'.

Her husband died in 1965, aged 86. In 1998, when Sarah was 117, family members walked into her dining room and told her she had become the world's oldest living person. She smiled and said: 'So what?' The following year, on 30 December, one of the carers at the Allentown nursing home where Sarah lived called in to check on her. She was fine, and showed no sign of any illness. Less than an hour later another check was made: Sarah had passed away. By just 33 hours she had missed out on becoming one of the very few people to live in three centuries. She left many descendants, including one great-great-great-grandson, four-year-old Bradley.

One person who might have overtaken Sarah Knauss was Violet Brown, who died in 2017 at the age of 117. Her birth on 10 March 1900 in Jamaica (then still owned by Britain) made her Queen Victoria's last surviving subject. Her first child, Harland Fairweather, had died earlier in 2017 at the age of 97. He was believed to be the oldest person with a living parent.

SCIENCE/TECHNOLOGY

◆

Linus Pauling: second person to receive a second Nobel Prize

Marie Curie won her second Nobel Prize in 1911. It took half a century, but eventually in 1962 someone repeated the feat. The American Linus Pauling (Nobel Laureate in Chemistry in 1954) won the Peace Prize.

Pauling first became interested in chemistry when a schoolfriend amazed him with the experiments possible using a small lab kit. He conducted his own experiments with equipment salvaged from a disused steel plant, then with another friend (Lloyd Simon) he set up Palmon Laboratories (a combination of their names). The schoolboys' business venture failed, but Pauling's enthusiasm continued. His pioneering research into the bonds between atoms was summed up in his book *The Nature of the Chemical Bond*. It has been cited as chemistry's most influential book of the 20th century, its 'effective bible'. Pauling's work, as well as his research into the structure of DNA (at around the same time as the more famous Watson and Crick), gained him the 1954 Nobel Prize in Chemistry.

But since World War II Pauling had also been a peace campaigner. At the beginning of the Manhattan Project

(America's attempt to develop a nuclear bomb), his friend Robert Oppenheimer had asked Pauling to lead the chemistry side of the task. Pauling declined, saying he didn't want to move his family. A more personal element to the two men's relationship – in fact the cause of its sudden end – was Oppenheimer calling round to Pauling's house when the scientist was at work so he could proposition Pauling's wife Ava. She rebuffed his advances and told her husband.

It was Ava's pacifism that influenced Pauling after the war, and he began to campaign against the development of nuclear weapons. His 1962 Nobel Peace Prize attracted criticism: some scientists saw him as furthering the cause of the Soviet Union, and *Life* magazine called the prize 'A Weird Insult from Norway'. The Nobel committee sits in Sweden.

A further two people have won a second Nobel Prize (the physicist John Bardeen and the chemist Frederick Sanger), but Pauling remains the only double-winner not to share either of his prizes with another person. An incidental result of his Peace Prize came from his high school. As a student 45 years previously, Pauling had asked his school principal if he could take two American history courses concurrently, during the spring semester: without these he wouldn't be eligible for his school diploma. The principal refused, meaning that Pauling left school without the diploma. In view of his two Nobel Prizes, however, the school now decided that he was worthy of it.

Curie remains the only woman to win two Nobel Prizes. She and Irène Joliot-Curie (who won the Prize in Chemistry in 1935) are the only mother-and-daughter winners. As of 2017, 48 women (compared to 844 men) have won Nobel Prizes. When Dorothy Hodgkin won the 1964 Prize in

Chemistry, the *Daily Mail*'s headline was 'British Wife Wins Nobel Prize'.

Helium: second element in the periodic table

Helium comes second to hydrogen not just in its atomic number (two, placing it second on the colourful table that adorns every school chemistry lab), but also in terms of its abundance. Although rare on Earth (it makes up just 5.2 parts per million in our atmosphere), helium is the second most common element in the observable universe, comprising 23 per cent of its mass.

One title the element can claim is lowest boiling point: minus 268.9 degrees Celsius. It is also the only element that will remain a liquid right down to absolute zero (minus 273.15 degrees Celsius). This makes it extremely useful in the field of cryogenics (the study of materials at very low temperatures). It helps in the cooling of superconducting magnets, as employed in MRI scanners.

Liquid helium displays some curious properties. Its refractive index makes its surface very hard to discern: styrofoam floats are often placed in it so observers can see where the surface is. It also 'creeps' out of containers, moving along the surface (even upwards) until it finds a warmer place, where it evaporates. Although this makes it very hard to store, it also makes helium useful for detecting possible leaks. Containers such as cryogenic tanks can be tested by putting helium in them – if there's a potential escape route, you can be sure the helium will find it.

The element was first detected when its spectral line was

spotted by the French astronomer Jules Janssen during a total solar eclipse in India in 1868. The British astronomer Norman Lockyer was the first to suggest that the line was due to a new element: he named it after Helios, the Greek god of the Sun. Much of the world's helium is to be found underneath the US, whose government established the National Helium Reserve in 1925 at Amarillo, Texas. They banned the element's export, which is why the German airship *Hindenburg* had to use hydrogen instead. Unlike helium, this gas is flammable, as the *Hindenburg* found out to its cost.

Another use is in deep-sea diving: helium's low molecular weight means that adding it to divers' tanks makes their air easier to breathe in. But of course, most of us encounter helium in the party balloons we like to inhale from to make our voices go squeaky. This effect happens because the speed of sound in the gas is three times that in air: the actual frequency of our voices doesn't change (that's dictated by the vibration of our vocal cords), just the timbre. You shouldn't overdo it, though: inhaling too much can be dangerous. In 1998 an Australian girl became unconscious and turned blue after inhaling the entire contents of a helium balloon.

Hook Lighthouse: second-oldest operating lighthouse in the world

The Tower of Hercules in north-west Spain has been around since Roman times, but at 800 or so years old Ireland's Hook Lighthouse is in second place. The exact date of the tower's construction is unknown. It was built by William Marshal, the 2nd Earl of Pembroke, who arrived in that part of Ireland in 1201. But it was definitely being shown on maps by 1240. Marshal had it constructed at the tip of County Wexford's Hook Peninsula so that ships could safely reach the town of New Ross, several miles upriver. Marshal was also one of the Magna Carta sureties (the men who guaranteed it would be enforced). His uncle Richard de Clare (known as Strongbow) was an ancestor of the Bush family, two of whom became US President.

Hook Head, the tip of the peninsula, gets its name either from the Old English word for a projecting piece of land or because its Irish name (Rinn Dubhain) sounds like *duan*, meaning 'fish hook'. At first the lighthouse (whose walls, up to 13 feet thick, contain several rooms, including two toilets) was manned by monks, who lit fires as warnings to sailors. They were replaced by lighthouse-keepers in the 17th century. Mariners continually complained about the poor quality of the coal fires, so in 1791 an oil lantern was installed, 12 feet in diameter and with 12 lamps. It burned whale oil. This was replaced in turn by gas lighting in 1871. Paraffin took over in 1911, and a clockwork mechanism was introduced which provided a flashing rather than a fixed light. The mechanism needed winding every 25 minutes by the keeper. Electricity finally arrived in 1972, and in 1996 the lighthouse was converted to automatic operation, allowing the final keepers to leave. The tower is now remotely controlled by the Irish Lighthouse Authority, which with a certain poetry is known as the 'Commissioners of Irish Lights'.

For a long time the lighthouse also operated fog warnings. At first these were guns (fired every ten minutes), then explosive charges, and more recently a compressed air horn.

In 2011 the fog warnings came to an end, as modern naval technology had rendered them unnecessary.

Hook Head is near the village of Crooke – this has been cited as a possible explanation of the phrase 'by hook or by crook'.

Royal Liver Building: second-biggest clock face in Britain

Just 2 centimetres (less than an inch) is the margin here. Each of the four clocks on Liverpool's Royal Liver Building measures 7.6 metres in diameter, while the one on London's 80 Strand building is 7.62 metres. (The building subsequently housed the publishers Penguin, but used to be the UK HQ of the Shell oil company, which is why the clock was once nicknamed 'Big Benzene'.) The Liverpool clocks may be smaller, but they are also older, dating from 1911. In fact they were originally known as the George clocks, because they were started on 22 June that year at the exact moment George V was crowned. They were made by the Gent Company of Leicester. Before the clock faces were sent to Liverpool, 39 guests were seated around one of them to enjoy a banquet. A photo was taken of the event, and another of 11 men standing behind one of the minute hands perched horizontally on stands. The hand is 14 feet long, and 3 feet at its widest part. The four pairs of hands, with their bearing spindles, weigh 2 tons.

The Liver Building was constructed as the home of Royal Liver Assurance, a friendly society originally founded to 'provide for the decent interment of deceased members'. The building is famous for the two statues of liver birds (officially cormorants) that perch atop its towers. They have names: Bella looks out to sea to keep watch over the boats arriving into port, while Bertie faces inland to protect the people of Liverpool. Or, if you believe some Scousers, Bella is keeping an eye out for good-looking sailors while Bertie is waiting to see if the pubs are open. Local legend says that should the birds ever fly away, the city will fall. A liver bird features in Liverpool's coat of arms (with seaweed in its beak), and also in the coat of arms of Paul McCartney (holding a guitar). The statues (each of which has a 24-foot wingspan) were designed by Carl Bernard Bartels, and constructed by the Bromsgrove Guild, the company of artists whose most famous works are the main gates at Buckingham Palace.

The Liver Building was bought in 2017 by a consortium that included Farhad Moshiri, the majority shareholder of Everton Football Club. He wanted to have his office in the building, looking out to the club's proposed new stadium at Bramley Moore Dock.

Clocks, incidentally, are a very suitable category for a book on seconds. The second gets its name precisely because it's the second division of an hour. The *secunda minuta* (literally, 'second minute') is a subdivision of the 'prime minute' – the minute itself.

Westminster Bridge: second bridge in central London

It took several centuries for one of the world's greatest cities to get a second bridge across its river. This was largely because the first one was determined to see off any competition. London Bridge (in its various incarnations) had stood in the City of London since Roman times, and whenever another crossing was proposed the Corporation of London (the City's governing body) objected. They were aided by the watermen (the boat operators), who argued that a new bridge would cost them their jobs and there would then be a lack of readily available seamen ready to serve in the navy should England go to war. In 1664 the Corporation granted a loan of £100,000 to Charles II, thanking him for preventing 'the new bridge proposed to be built over the river of Thames betwixt Lambeth and Westminster, which, as it is conceived, would have been of dangerous consequence to the state of this City'. That is 'loan', then, used in the sense of 'bribe'.

But by 1736 the need for improved links between the expanding West End and south London (not to mention the south-coast ports) could be ignored no longer. Parliamentary approval was granted for a bridge at Westminster, and funding was raised by lottery, which led the writer Henry Fielding to dub the project 'the Bridge of Fools'. The designer chosen was Charles Labelye of Switzerland. This caused resentment among English architects: the surveyor Batty Langley published a pamphlet entitled *Survey of Westminster Bridge as 'tis now sinking into ruin*, which called Labelye 'Mr Self-Sufficient' and pictured him hanging from his own bridge. (Langley liked a dramatic touch – he named four of his sons Hiram, Euclid, Vitruvius and Archimedes.) This was unfair on Labelye, who during his work on the bridge invented the caisson (a watertight structure that lets work continue in the dry), which is used to this day.

The structure, built of Portland stone, was opened on 18 November 1750. *The Gentleman's Magazine* described it as 'a very great ornament to our metropolis, and will be looked on with pleasure or envy by all foreigners. The surprising echo in the arches, brings much company with French horns to entertain themselves under it in summer.' This wasn't the only entertainment on offer: the semi-octagonal turrets along the bridge, intended to give shelter to pedestrians, soon became home to prostitutes. James Boswell (the biographer of Samuel Johnson) recorded in his diary for Tuesday 10 May 1763: 'At the bottom of the Haymarket I picked up a strong, jolly young damsel, and taking her under the arm I conducted her to Westminster Bridge, and then in armour complete did I engage her upon this noble edifice. The whim of doing it there with the Thames rolling below us amused me much.' Rather different from William Wordsworth's peaceful crossing of the bridge on 3 September 1802, which inspired his famous poem about the view, beginning 'Earth has not anything to show more fair'.

The competition offered by the new bridge led the City of London to remove the buildings on London Bridge in order to make it wider. They also built Blackfriars Bridge, which opened in 1769. But the early criticism of Labelye's work eventually proved justified: by the mid-19th century Westminster Bridge had started to subside, and a replacement had to be built. This was on the same site as the original structure but twice as wide. So the first half was built while the existing bridge remained in use, then the other half added afterwards, so removing the need for a temporary bridge. This second second bridge (as it were) was opened on 24 May 1862, Queen Victoria's 43rd birthday. She was due to perform the ceremony herself, but withdrew as she was still in mourning for her husband Albert, who had died the previous December. The bridge is still in use today, making it the oldest road bridge in central London. It also has seven arches, more than any other bridge across the Thames.

Coincidentally, 1862 was also the year that Lambeth Bridge opened. This finally signalled the end of the horse ferry that had operated on that site for centuries, and which gave its name to nearby Horseferry Road (where the famous magistrates' court stands, and where Phyllis Pearsall lived in a bedsit as she compiled the first *London A to Z*.) The ferry wasn't actually operated by a horse pulling a rope along the shore – it was a conventional one, the name arising from the fact that it was large enough to pull horses and carriages. This ferry's pier was where James II began his escape from England in 1689.

Today Lambeth Bridge is painted red, while Westminster Bridge is painted green – because they are respectively at the Lords and Commons ends of Parliament.

Shanghai Tower: second-tallest building in the world

The 2,073-foot tower in the Pudong district of Shanghai might not be a record-holder, but it is clever – it twists through 120 degrees as it rises, so reducing the effect of high winds on the structure. And in one respect the Chinese building *does* beat Dubai's Burj Khalifa (at 2,717 feet the tallest building in the world): it has the planet's furthest-travelling lift, covering 1,898 feet. That's taller than the entire height of New York's One World Trade Center (the replacement for the buildings destroyed on 9/11).

For a long time New York itself ruled the skyscraper scene.

A previous holder of the title of second-tallest building on the planet was 40 Wall Street, which during the early months of 1930 raced the Chrysler Building, also in Manhattan, to see who could bag the world record. Although they were 4 miles apart, the two construction sites were visible to each other simply because of their height. At one point the architects of 40 Wall Street redrew their plans to beat the Chrysler's published figure, and indeed briefly – very briefly – they did outgrow their rival. But the builders of the Chrysler had constructed their now famous (though then secret) spire inside the structure. After 40 Wall Street had been completed, and its owners were celebrating what they assumed was victory, the Chrysler team pushed their spire up into place, so snatching the crown.

They didn't get long in the limelight, though. The following year the Empire State Building appeared a few blocks to the west, forcing the Chrysler into second place. Third position was soon occupied by 70 Pine Street – which incorporates the charming feature of a 3D scale model of itself just above the main entrance.

District Line: second line on the London Underground

On Christmas Eve 1868, five years after the Metropolitan Railway had become London's (indeed the world's) first underground train line, it was joined by the Metropolitan District Railway (known today as the District Line). It was instantly clear that these two routes – one covering the main Euston and Marylebone Roads, the other the Embankment along the Thames – could be joined together by short sections of track to form a 'circular' line that enclosed central London. This is how they operate today, but such was the animosity between the two companies' chairmen that it was well over a decade before the Circle Line became a reality.

Edward Watkin, head of the Metropolitan, probably wouldn't have taken kindly to anyone trying to share his place in the limelight. He was, shall we say, a determined character. He once tried to build a rival to the Eiffel Tower at Wembley, to attract customers onto his train line. Construction reached the first stage, but the structure never gained many visitors, and it was soon abandoned. (Eventually, now known as Watkin's Folly, it began to tilt to one side and had to be pulled down.) Watkin was similarly ambitious for the Metropolitan Line itself: he wanted to extend it to Paris. Trains would proceed to the Kent coast, where they would descend in enormous lifts to a tunnel that ran underneath the Channel to France. This was nearly a century before Eurostar, and officialdom wasn't ready for the idea. The War Office argued that such a tunnel would allow foreigners to invade Britain. Watkin replied that he'd thought of that: he would lay explosive charges along the tunnel's length, allowing it to be blown up at the touch of a button. The authorities politely declined to discuss the idea any further.

James Forbes, boss of the District Line, didn't warm to Watkin either. For years the two men delayed planners' attempts to get them working together, so it was 1884 before the Circle Line started running. At the opening banquet Forbes claimed that the arguments between him and Watkin had been 'only slight' – but even as he spoke, Watkin was sitting next to him making notes for his solicitors about the pair's next dispute. Services started operating, but still the antagonism continued. The Metropolitan ran the clockwise trains, the District the anti-clockwise ones – but neither would tell you, at their separate ticket offices, that services in the other direction were available. With 27 stations on the line, passengers sometimes found that after buying their ticket they had to travel, say, 24 stations in the wrong direction rather than three in the right direction. The Circle was electrified in 1905 – predictably the two companies used different systems which proved incompatible, resulting in further delays.

Today, the District Line can claim at least one record: it has 60 stations, more than any other Tube line.

Budapest Metro: second underground train system in the world

The race to follow London into the transport history books was a close one. The Hungarian capital won it by just six months, opening the first line of its metro system on 3 May 1896. Just seven months later, on 14 December, Glasgow opened its subway. But the Scots can comfort themselves with the fact that their system has the cooler nickname: because of its circular route and the colour of its trains it is known as the Clockwork Orange.

R34 airship: the second transatlantic non-stop flight

During World War I, the British government commissioned airships for military use. But by the time the R34 was completed, the war was over. So the Admiralty let the Air Ministry use it for experiments in air travel. One ambition was a non-stop flight across the Atlantic, and if it hadn't been for damage suffered during testing, the R34 might have been the first to achieve the goal. As it was, John Alcock and Arthur Brown grabbed the honour, flying a Vickers Vimy plane from Newfoundland to Ireland in June 1919.

Just two weeks later the R34 set off on its own journey. There were 30 people on board, sleeping in hammocks slung up across walkways, their food stored in lockers that had replaced the bomb racks. Hot food was prepared with the help of a plate welded to an engine exhaust pipe. A northerly route was followed, so that the airship would never be too far from land in the event of an emergency.

A gramophone played jazz records, which may or may not have soothed the nerves of the wireless operators getting electrostatic shocks from the equipment. At two o'clock on the first afternoon, crew member William Ballantyne – who had been told there wasn't room for him on the flight – was discovered hiding between the girders and gasbags in the hull of the ship, together with the crew's mascot, a cat called Whoopsie. Ballantyne had intended to hide for the whole trip, but the smell of gas made him nauseous and forced him out. Had they been over land the officers in charge would have forced him to jump out with a parachute. As it was he was forced to peel potatoes and hand-pump petrol into the tanks for the rest of the journey.

At one point Brigadier-General Edward Maitland looked down and became the first man to see an iceberg from the air. He noticed the underwater section, which 'could, under no circumstances, be seen from a surface ship'. Coming only a few years after the sinking of the *Titanic*, the thought was a sobering one.

There were minor issues like a cracked water cylinder jacket (repaired with the aid of chewing gum), but the only serious problem came as the R34 approached its intended landing site on New York's Long Island. Fuel levels were running dangerously low: every drop was drained from every tank and poured into the main tanks so the engine could keep running. The handling party waiting for them on the ground had no experience of such large airships, so Major E.M. Pritchard parachuted down from the R34 to offer advice. He thereby became the first man to arrive in America from Europe by air.

After its flight of 108 hours the ship landed with enough petrol for only another 40 minutes. The crew were treated as heroes in New York, so much so that when they set off for their return journey four days later they made a point of flying over Manhattan before turning back towards the Atlantic and home. Whoopsie was again on board, despite a Broadway actress having offered $1,000 for the cat.

William Ballantyne, however, had to make his own arrangements.

Pegasus: second-tallest statue in the US

In 2014, as part of improvement works at Gulfstream Park racetrack in Hallandale Beach, Florida, a huge statue was unveiled of Pegasus, the winged horse of Greek mythology. Its front-left foot is stamping down on a dragon. The dragon is 50 feet high, but Pegasus rises 110 feet into the air, putting him second only to the Statue of Liberty (151 feet from head to toe). Pegasus, the largest statue of a horse in the world, contains 330 tons of steel and 132 tons of bronze. It was made in China, then shipped to Florida in 23 packing containers, 40 Chinese workers following to put it back together. Its steel beams arrived from Germany, and the whole project cost $30m. It sits amid a musical fountain show (according to legend, wherever Pegasus stamped his foot a spring would appear), which has LED lighting and makes the dragon breathe 20-foot flames.

The statue was the idea of Gulfstream's owner. Pegasus is an obvious fit for a horse-racing track (it's also said the statue represents good prevailing over evil), and follows in a long tradition. During World War II Britain's newly formed Parachute Regiment adopted Pegasus (ridden by the warrior Bellerophon) as their insignia, to symbolise them arriving into battle by air. The bridge over the Caen Canal which they captured ahead of D-Day has been known ever since as Pegasus Bridge, and the course you have to pass to join the Paras is run by Pegasus Company. The creature also features as the emblem of the Inner Temple (one of the Inns of Court to which barristers belong in England and Wales), TriStar Pictures, the American version of *Reader's Digest* and Mobil Oil. The Taiwanese computer manufacturer AsusTek took their name from Pegasus, omitting the first three letters so they would appear first in telephone directories.

Some neighbours of the Florida Pegasus, however, are less than happy about the statue. Houses to the north have a view of its anatomically correct backside, while a local real-estate broker commented: 'Nothing says "Welcome to

Gulfstream Park" better than a horse stomping on a lizard that was made in China.'

One Canada Square: second-tallest building in the UK

In the dying days of his premiership, in an attempt to fend off the oblivion he sensed was coming his way at the 1997 general election, John Major undertook a tour of important people at the main national newspapers. This included a trip to One Canada Square, home to the Mirror Group, where Kelvin MacKenzie (once editor of the *Sun*) was by then working. MacKenzie's office was high up in what was then the UK's tallest building. 'Quite a view you've got from here,' said the Prime Minister. 'Yes,' replied MacKenzie. 'On a clear day you can almost see a Tory voter.'

Since then One Canada Square has been overtaken by the Shard. But at 770 feet the tower still dominates the area of London known as Canary Wharf, so much so that it is often mistakenly called 'Canary Wharf' itself. That title for the northern part of the Isle of Dogs comes from the warehouse built there in 1937 by Fruit Lines Limited, a company that imported fruit from the Canary Islands. The area had long been associated with shipping, a history now reflected in a series of mosaics set into the floor of Jubilee Place, one of Canary Wharf's shopping malls. Among the information they contain is the fact that in 1858 a rope used in the launch of the *Great Eastern* was almost 4 feet in circumference.

Perhaps the 'Canary Wharf' mistake is so common because the first three letters coincide with those of 'Canada Square'. The square's name denotes the site's Canadian developers, Olympia and York. They originally wanted to clad the landmark building in stone, but their architect Cesar Pelli (also responsible for the Petronas Towers in Kuala Lumpur) argued for steel, to reflect Britain's industrial past. Pelli showed a model of his building to Prince Charles, who replied: 'I personally would go mad if I had to work in a place like that.' The rejuvenation of the docks was seen as totemic of the 1980s boom presided over by Margaret Thatcher, and although One Canada Square itself wasn't finished until after she had left office, it still attracted the nickname 'Thatcher's cock'.

The tower has 4,388 steps and 32 lifts. Avoiding them all, the Frenchman Alain 'Spiderman' Robert climbed the outside of the building all the way to the top in 2002. The distinctive stainless-steel pyramid at the summit is 130 feet tall and 98 feet square. Like all skyscrapers, One Canada Square is designed to cope with high winds: its tuned mass damper (a large pendulum-like device) means it can sway up to 13 inches. The 3,960 windows can be cleaned manually or by a machine that runs on rails fixed to the building: it can complete a window in 2.6 seconds, and if it does the whole tower consumes 426,000 gallons of water. The 13th floor contains no office space, only air-conditioning equipment – the owners insist this is a coincidence, and not a way of avoiding the well-known superstition.

One Canada Square was opened by the Duke of Edinburgh on 26 August 1991. There was a recession at the time, meaning that initial take-up of office space in the tower was very low. (Exactly the same thing had happened with the Empire State Building 60 years previously, leading to it being known as the 'Empty State Building'.) To maintain interest in One Canada Square, in October 1992 its owners opened a public observation deck on the 50th floor. However, this closed after just a few weeks, following an attempt by the IRA to bomb the tower. The attempt failed: the terrorists attracted the attention of a security guard by parking the van containing the bomb on a double yellow line.

SPACE

❖

Saturn: second-biggest planet in the Solar System

With a diameter of 75,335 miles, Saturn might feel inferior to Jupiter (87,388 miles). But it dwarfs every other planet in the Solar System: the next-biggest, Uranus, comes in at a paltry 31,702 miles. If Saturn were an empty shell, you could fit 763 Earths inside it. Between them, Jupiter and Saturn comprise 92 per cent of the Solar System's total planetary mass.

But despite its size, Saturn has a very low density. About three-quarters of it is hydrogen, and almost all of the rest is helium. Indeed it's the only planet less dense than water – which means that if you could find a big enough bath, Saturn would float in it.

The planet has been seen with the naked eye since ancient times, but the first person to observe it with a telescope was Galileo in 1610. Its yellow appearance is due to the ammonia crystals in its upper atmosphere. Apart from its size, Saturn has a couple of other second places in the Solar System. At 1,100 miles per hour its winds are the second-fastest (after Neptune's), and its largest moon, Titan, is the second-largest. Such is Saturn's size that Titan is bigger than the planet Mercury.

Because Saturn is named after the Roman god of agriculture, its astrological symbol is a sickle. The Greek writer Claudius Ptolemy called it 'lord of the right ear, the spleen, the bladder, the phlegm and the bones'. Astrologers traditionally associated it with slowness and gloom, so these qualities have come to be marked by the adjective 'saturnine'. In Roman astrology Saturn was thought to control the first hour of the sixth day of the week, so that day was named after it – hence our modern 'Saturday'. And the rockets that launched NASA's astronauts towards the Moon were named Saturn as they were the successors to the Jupiter series.

The gap between two of Saturn's sets of rings is known as the Cassini Division, after the scientist Giovanni Cassini who discovered it at the Paris Observatory in 1675. Cassini's work on longitude also allowed an accurate measurement of the size of France. The country was found to be smaller than previously thought, prompting Louis XIV to say that Cassini had taken away more of his kingdom than he himself had added to it with all his wars.

Alan Shepard: second person in space

Given the US military's love of acronyms, it was surely tempting fate to call their attempt to beat the Russians at the ultimate journey 'Man in Space Soonest'. But miss is exactly what they did: on 12 April 1961 Yuri Gagarin became the first person to travel into space. It was, however, a very close-run thing.

The American effort was begun by the US Air Force, then in 1958 handed over to the newly formed National

Aeronautics and Space Administration. NASA re-christened it Project Mercury (after the winged messenger of the Roman gods). The following year Alan Shepard was one of seven military test pilots chosen as the nation's first team of astronauts. Five of the 'Mercury Seven' (including Shepard) would go on to give their names to the pilots in the TV series *Thunderbirds*.

On 18 May 1959 the team gathered at Cape Canaveral to watch the launch of their first rocket, an SM-65D Atlas. After just 64 seconds of flight it exploded. Shepard turned to fellow astronaut John Glenn and said: 'Well, I'm glad they got that out of the way.' But by January 1961 a successful manned space flight was looking a serious possibility. Shepard was picked ahead of the other six as the man to make it. He told his wife Louise: 'Lady, you can't tell anyone, but you have your arms around the man who'll be first in space!' She replied: 'Who let a Russian in here?' Shepard laughed, but was all too aware of 'those Russian boosters rolling to their pads'.

Despite the pressure – and Shepard's impatience to go ahead – NASA insisted on performing a test flight with a chimpanzee on board. This was completed on 31 January, with the chimp splashing down successfully in the Atlantic having suffered only a bruised nose. He was given the name Ham, because he had lived at the Holloman Aerospace Medical Center in New Mexico (though this title was only awarded after the flight, as officials didn't want to find themselves reporting the death of a named animal). But the craft had landed 132 miles off-target, so NASA ordered another unmanned test.

This happened in March. Gagarin made it into space in

April. As Shepard would write later, he'd have won the race 'if only the damn chimp's ride had been on the mark'. Nevertheless Project Mercury continued, and on 5 May Shepard followed the trail blazed by his Russian counterpart. Asked what he'd been thinking about as he waited to launch, he replied: 'The fact that every part of this ship was built by the lowest bidder.' After being recovered from the Atlantic he said: 'It's not the fall that hurts – it's the sudden stop.'

Shepard's subsequent career was chequered. He was diagnosed with Ménière's disease, an ear condition causing dizziness and nausea. This grounded him for most of the 1960s. But by 1969, having undergone surgery, he was reinstated to full flight status, and took his place in the queue to visit the Moon. At one point he was lined up to command Apollo 13, but it was decided he needed more training – a lucky escape, as the mission had to abort its Moon landing and was nearly fatal for the three men on board.

In the end Shepard made his Moonwalk on 5–6 February 1971, as part of the Apollo 14 mission. He was the oldest Moonwalker (47), and the only one who admitted to the experience making him cry. But he is most famous for becoming the only man to play golf on the Moon. He first had the idea when Bob Hope was given a tour of NASA: the comedian had a club with him. Apollo regulations forbade any unnecessary weight, so Shepard had to smuggle his collapsible 6-iron and two golf balls on board in his sock. His lunar suit made a proper swing on the Moon rather difficult, and he scuffed his first shot. But he connected properly with the second one, sending it (in his words) 'miles and miles and miles'. Actually it was later estimated at between 200 and 400 yards.

Today Shepard's club is to be found at the United States Golf Association Museum in New Jersey. As is his sock.

Apollo 12: second mission to land on the Moon

Apollo 12 is the ultimate second. If you want a story that hardly anyone knows, that deserves far more attention than it gets, that remains in the shadow of a more famous but less interesting predecessor, then Apollo 12 is the story for you.

Pete Conrad and Alan Bean were, in their very different ways, far more engaging characters than Neil Armstrong and Buzz Aldrin. Conrad was the wisecracking, happy-go-lucky US Air Force pilot who was destined for greatness, a gap-toothed hero famous around NASA for his one-liners. Forced (against his nature) to take part in Rorschach inkblot tests as part of the astronaut selection programme, he told the psychiatrist that one card, deliberately left blank, was 'upside down'. Conrad was also famed for always wearing a baseball cap. He had a huge one made that would fit over his space helmet, which he was going to wear on the lunar surface to surprise NASA officials watching back on Earth. Unfortunately he couldn't smuggle it on board the spacecraft.

Alan Bean was the quieter of the two. Not considered an outstanding pilot, he was rejected in an early round of NASA selection, and only got the chance to go to the Moon because another astronaut was killed in a plane crash. But Bean didn't mind: 'When you see other people achieving success and you're not, you say, "What is it? Is it talent or is it something else?" You don't want it to be talent, because then you're stuck. I always wanted to do something you can accomplish with determination and persistence.' Bean's concentration on the task was so total that in the final few months before the mission he deliberately forgot people's names as soon as he was introduced to them at parties, in case the information pushed out of his memory something he needed for the Moon trip.

Apollo 12 launched from Kennedy Space Center in Florida on 14 November 1969, four months after Armstrong and Aldrin's Moonwalk. After 36 seconds the craft was hit by lightning. The electrical systems were soon up and running again, but the possibility remained that the parachutes (which would let the capsule splash back into the ocean at the end of the mission) had been damaged. Should the mission be aborted? It was decided that if the parachutes were going to fail, they'd fail just as fatally now as after the crew had been to the Moon and back. As Alan Bean put it: 'If [the] parachutes don't work then, well – at least [we've] had ten days in a great adventure.'

On the way to the Moon the crew (Conrad, Bean and Dick Gordon, who would stay in orbit while the other two descended to the lunar surface) danced weightlessly to 'Sugar Sugar' by the Archies. On 19 November Pete Conrad became the third man to walk on the Moon. His first words were: 'Whoopie! Man, that may have been a small one for Neil, but that's a long one for me.' At only 5 feet 6 inches he was shorter than Armstrong, so his drop from the ladder was greater. He had arranged those words with a journalist who had said she didn't believe that NASA let the astronauts choose their own words. Betting her $500 that that was what he would say, Conrad duly delivered the words. He never received his money.

Conrad became both the first man to dance on the Moon and the first man to fall over on the Moon. Alan Bean, on the other hand, was in charge of the TV camera that would deliver pictures back to Earth. Unlike Apollo 11's this was colour rather than black and white – but unfortunately the first thing Bean did was point it straight towards the Sun, burning it out and ensuring that only still pictures would be possible. Though not the picture Bean had hoped for: he'd managed to sneak a self-timer device on board, and was planning to take a photo of himself and Conrad together on the Moon, which would have prompted officials back on Earth to ask who'd taken it. But when it came to it he couldn't find the device, and the photo remained an idea. However, Bean did become the first man to eat spaghetti on the Moon (he was known for eating it all the time on Earth), and also threw his silver astronaut badge into the lunar dust, where it remains to this day. Silver badges were awarded to astronauts in training, but only those who flew in space got the gold ones – Bean knew he would no longer need his lesser badge.

Back on Earth the two friends proved to be among the more well-adjusted Moonwalkers. Pete Conrad never let the experience define his life, saying of some of the other ten in the club that 'they never came back'. Alan Bean found that his visit to Earth's satellite only made him more interested in Earth itself. He would go and sit in shopping malls just to 'watch the people go by. I'd think, boy, why do people complain about the Earth? We are living in the Garden of Eden. Since [my Moonwalk] I have not complained about the weather one single time. I'm glad there *is* weather. I've not complained about traffic – I'm glad there are people around.'

When people found out that Conrad had been to the Moon they – inevitably – asked him what it was like, a discussion he would avert with a simple: 'Super!' But very few people *did* find out. At a party to celebrate the 20th anniversary of the Pink Floyd album *Dark Side of the Moon*, to which Conrad and Buzz Aldrin had been invited, a young waiter tried to tell Conrad – not knowing who he was – that there *was* no dark side (that the Moon rotated in such a way that people on Earth got to see all of it). Conrad corrected him, adding: 'Trust me, I've been there.' In the mid-1970s Conrad shot a commercial for American Express, part of a series of ads the credit-card company was running featuring 'famous' people that no one recognised. Conrad said he was recognised far more after the advert than he had been after going to the Moon.

After leaving NASA, Alan Bean had a successful career as an artist. His paintings sold for hundreds of thousands of dollars. He died in May 2018, aged 86. Peter Conrad had died in 1999, aged 69. Having made it safely to the moon and back, he met his end in a motorbike accident.

Svetlana Savitskaya: second woman in space

Considering the astonishing speed with which space exploration developed in the 1960s, it's hard to believe it took 19 years for someone to follow the lead of Valentina Tereshkova, the first woman in space. Tereshkova piloted Russia's Vostok

6 in 1963. It wasn't until 1982 that Svetlana Savitskaya flew aboard Soyuz T-7 to the Salyut 7 space station. (It would take a further year after that for Sally Ride to become the third woman, and the first American woman, in space.)

Savitskaya had the genes for adventure – her father, Yevgeniy Savitzky, had been a fighter ace during World War II. She went on to be one of the five cosmonauts who raised the Russian flag at the Sochi Winter Olympics in 2014 – only fitting for someone who (on her second flight in 1984) had become the first woman to perform a spacewalk, and the first woman to weld metal in space.

A UFO event involving a physical effect: a close encounter of the second kind

A rare case of a second being put in the shade by its third rather than its first. In 1972 J. Allen Hynek, an American astrophysicist who had previously specialised in the study of spectroscopic binary stars and early US satellites, published a book called *The UFO Experience: A Scientific Inquiry*. After early scepticism he had become convinced that some UFO sightings deserved further investigation, and wrote the book in an attempt to introduce scientific rigour to the process. He suggested that 'close encounters' should be classified in three different groups. The first would be sightings less than 500 feet away, while the second would be events involving a physical effect (impressions in the ground, a chemical trace, interference in the functioning of an electronic device or the like). The third kind would be encounters in which an alien creature was actually present.

This last category was the one that got Steven Spielberg thinking. Hynek ended up with an uncredited cameo in *Close Encounters of the Third Kind* – smoking a pipe, he steps forward to view the abductees released from the aliens' spaceship.

POLITICS/INSTITUTIONS

◆

Earl of Wilmington: second Prime Minister of Great Britain

Robert Walpole is always highlighted in lists of British prime ministers, both as the first (he became PM in 1721), and the longest-serving (over 20 years). So the fact that his immediate successor is never remembered is understandable – but not entirely fair.

Spencer Compton (as he was born) was elected as an MP in 1698, first for Eye in Suffolk, later for East Grinstead. In 1715 he became Speaker of the House of Commons. He once interrupted an MP (the Duke of Newcastle) during a speech. The Duke complained that he was entitled to finish his comments. 'No sir,' replied Compton, 'you have a right to speak, but the House have a right to judge whether they will hear you.'

He was also Treasurer to the Prince of Wales, and was hoping to get the nod as Prime Minister when his boss succeeded to the throne as George II in 1727. Back then it was customary for a change of monarch to be accompanied by a change of political rule. But Walpole formed an alliance with the new King's wife, Caroline, ensuring that he stayed on as PM. The two worked together while allowing the King to think he was in charge. Compton was compensated by being elevated to the House of Lords: he became Baron (later the Earl of) Wilmington.

Eventually, after the death of Caroline, Walpole lost his influence, and had to resign in 1742. The most obvious successor as PM was Edward Carteret, but George II preferred to promote his former employee Wilmington. However, real power was exercised by Carteret, from his position as Northern Secretary. The only Act of Parliament passed during Wilmington's year and a half in the job was the Place Bill, which limited the number of offices an MP could hold. Londoners were much more excited by 1742's big development, the city's first indoor swimming pool (the Bagnio in Whitechapel).

The following year Britain fought France in the Battle of Dettingen. George II led the troops into battle, the last time a British monarch would do so. Wilmington was also present, but stayed well away from the fighting, sitting in a coach. Already in poor health, he died in London just a few days later, on 2 July. He was unmarried and had no children. But his name lives on in Wilmington, Delaware, and there are also Wilmingtons in North Carolina and Vermont. His memory survived as well in London's Foundling Hospital, the home for abandoned children that he helped to institute.

But perhaps his most wide-reaching legacy is Compton Wynyates, the family seat in Warwickshire (where Wilmington had been born and where he is buried). The house has featured in several movies – including an appearance as a monastery in *Carry on Camping* – and was the inspiration for Croft Manor, the childhood home of Lara Croft in the *Tomb Raider* video games.

Richard Onslow: second Speaker of the House of Commons

When Great Britain was formed in 1707, its House of Commons was presided over by John Smith. His successor, taking office the following year, was Richard Onslow. Both his father and grandfather had been politicians, the latter (Thomas Foote) serving as Lord Mayor of London in 1649. Perhaps it was this that led Onslow to take an overly detailed interest in the technicalities of political life. Whatever the reason, he became known – and disliked – for his pedantic approach to the job. For example, when he led MPs to the House of Lords to hear their judgement in the trial of a preacher, he delayed proceedings by challenging Black Rod on an arcane point of privilege, infuriating everyone who was there. Because of this reputation he earned the nickname 'Stiff Dick'.

Thomas Townshend: second Home Secretary

The post of Home Secretary – or, more correctly, 'Her Majesty's Principal Secretary of State for the Home Department' – was created in 1782. The Earl of Shelburne held the job for the first three months, but when the Prime Minister, the Marquess of Rockingham, died suddenly on 1 July, Shelburne succeeded him in the top job. He was replaced as Home Secretary by Thomas Townshend.

Born in Norfolk in 1733, Townshend was the grandson of the man whose agricultural innovations had earned him the nickname 'Turnip Townshend' (he was actually the 2nd

Viscount Townshend). On his way up the political ladder Thomas served a year as Clerk of the Green Cloth, the official who organised royal journeys (and whose table was covered in said material). The year after becoming Home Secretary he was made a member of the House of Lords. At first – and in spite of his period serving the royal family – he chose a title in honour of a relative of his, Algernon Sidney, who had campaigned against the monarchy increasing its power. But then Thomas worried that other members of his family might have a stronger claim on the 'Sidney' title, so veered towards 'Sydenham', after the village near his home in Kent. Finally he combined the two, compromising on the spelling and becoming known as the 1st Viscount Sydney.

His first spell as Home Secretary ended in April 1783, but in December of the same year he resumed in the post, and served until 1789. At this time the job also included responsibility for Britain's colonies (the title of Colonial Secretary having been recently abolished after the loss of America). As such the new Viscount Sydney was in charge of the policy of transporting convicts to Botany Bay in Australia. This is how the country's most famous city ended up bearing his name.

Townshend died in 1800. In 1915 his Kent home, Frognal House – which in the 1600s had been the largest in the area, boasting no fewer than 24 chimneys – was sold by the family to the government, who during World War I used it as the country's major hospital for facial and plastic surgery.

Margaret Wintringham: second woman to take her seat in the House of Commons

Nancy Astor is as famous for her verbal jousting with Winston Churchill as for being the first woman in the House of Commons. (Constance Markievicz had been elected in 1918, but, like all Sinn Fein representatives, refused to take her seat.) When Churchill complained that encountering a woman in Parliament was like having one intrude on him in the bathroom, Astor replied: 'Sir, you are not handsome enough to have such fears.' But what's less well known is the friendship Astor formed with the second woman to inhabit the green benches.

Thomas Wintringham, the Liberal MP for Louth, died of a heart attack in the House of Commons Library in August 1921. The local party asked his widow Margaret whether she would stand in the by-election. A headmistress and magistrate, she was a leading light in many movements, from the British Temperance Association to the Women's Institute. She had founded many branches of the latter, often driving potential new members to meetings. In the back of her car was an enormous teapot – she disliked the urns used by the WI.

Wintringham agreed to defend the seat, on one condition: because she was in mourning she would not speak at campaign meetings. (It is possible that this idea actually came from the party itself, to attract a sympathy vote.) Margaret attended the meetings, but the speaking was done by other people, including her two sisters and members of the National Union of Societies for Equal Citizenship. Support was also expressed by Lady Astor, who despite being a Conservative wanted to see more women in Parliament.

Farmers in the rural constituency doubted that a female MP could represent them properly. Nevertheless Margaret won the by-election in September. Standing on the balcony of Louth Town Hall she declared: 'Working among the people of Louth during the last few weeks has been like many bottles of medicine to me.' The following month, still dressed in black, she took her seat.

Wintringham and Astor soon formed a close friendship, the aristocratic Tory entertaining the more humble Liberal at her Buckinghamshire stately home, Cliveden. Margaret called Nancy the 'prancing pony' of the relationship, labelling herself the 'slow old carthorse'. When the pair were joined by another six women after the 1923 general election, Wintringham organised them in cross-party campaigns on issues such as equal pay for women and female-only train carriages.

Wintringham lost her seat at the 1924 general election, and never managed to re-enter Parliament. But her memory lives on even today. Victoria Atkins, who was elected for Louth and Horncastle at the 2015 general election, referred to her predecessor during her maiden speech: 'Mrs Wintringham ran a different campaign from my own, for she took a vow of silence and said not a word on the campaign trail – a difference that several constituents were keen to point out to me during the election.'

Arthur Henderson: second leader of the Labour Party

'Uncle Arthur', as he was affectionately known in the Labour movement, may not have been the first to lead his party

– that honour went to Keir Hardie – but he did become the first Labour Cabinet minister, and a turbulent history in the House of Commons also gave him joint ownership of one of the more unusual political records.

Henderson was born into a working-class Glasgow family in 1863, but when he was ten his father died, plunging the family into poverty. Arthur had to abandon his schooling and take a job in a foundry. Here he discovered a talent for debate and for representing his fellow workers, though he avoided conflict wherever possible, believing that strikes were usually counterproductive. Having moved to the north-east, in 1903 he became Mayor of Darlington. During his year in office he opened the town's electric tram system. The very first tram was driven by his wife.

Also in 1903 he was returned as MP for Barnard Castle. By 1906 the Labour Representation Committee had become the Labour Party, and at that year's general election Henderson and 28 others won seats in the House of Commons. Two years later Keir Hardie stood down, and Henderson assumed the party leadership. He resigned in 1910, but came back for a second spell in 1914. The following year he was appointed President of the Board of Education in Asquith's coalition government – the first Labour member of any Cabinet.

He then served as Minister without Portfolio under David Lloyd George, but when in August 1917 the Labour Party sent delegates to a socialist conference aimed at securing an end to the war, Lloyd George sacked him. Henderson learned of his dismissal in the press. He called this a 'shameful attack'.

His later positions in Labour governments included Home Secretary and Foreign Secretary, and he also served a third spell as leader of the party in 1931–2. In 1934 he was awarded the Nobel Peace Prize for his work in trying to avoid a second world war. He spent most of the time from 1903 to his death in 1935 as an MP, latterly with two of his three sons as colleagues (the third had been killed in World War I). But successive election defeats meant he had to work hard for this record, and indeed his count of four comebacks (representing five different constituencies), gives him the joint record with two other MPs. His occurred over the shortest time period – just 14 years.

Chancellor of the Exchequer: Second Lord of the Treasury

Troublesome Chancellors of the Exchequer tend to get re-minded that in the official Treasury rankings they only come second. There are several Lords Commissioners of Her Majesty's Treasury, acting as a group to exercise the ancient office of Lord High Treasurer. The Chancellor is Second Lord – the First Lord of the Treasury is the Prime Minister. And if the occupant of Number 11 Downing Street ever needs reminding of that, they have only to walk the few yards next door – the title is engraved on the Number 10 letterbox. There are several more junior Lords, usually members of the Government Whips office. The Chief Whip holds the title of Parliamentary Secretary to the Treasury.

The name 'Exchequer' derives from the checked tablecloth that was used by the state's financial office in medieval times. The table on which it was spread measured 10 feet by 5 feet, and had a raised edge to ensure nothing could fall off it. The cloth was black with green stripes (each about the width of a hand), so giving the appearance of a chess board (in French, *échiquier*). The squares designated pounds, shillings and pence, and the sums involved in tax and other transactions were represented by counters placed on the cloth.

As it happened, the second Chancellor of England, Sir John Maunsell (who took office in 1234), knew all about jobs involving cloth – his father, Walter, had at one point gloried in the title of Napkin Bearer to the King.

John Adams: second US President

The man who would succeed George Washington as leader of the United States was born in 1735 in Braintree, Massachusetts. His Puritan ancestors had come from England, believing (according to one modern writer) that 'they lived in the Bible. England under the Stuarts was Egypt; they were Israel fleeing . . . to establish a refuge for godliness, a city upon a hill.' As a young lawyer Adams used the pseudonym 'Humphrey Ploughjogger' to write press articles critical of British rule. While living in Boston – where, in a coincidental taste of things to come, his home was known as the 'White House' – he appeared in the court case arising from the Boston Massacre, where British soldiers killed five civilians. During this he used the phrase 'facts are stubborn things'.

America declared itself independent in 1776, and in 1785 Adams was appointed as its first Ambassador to Britain. When asked if he had any British relatives, he replied: 'Neither my father or mother, grandfather or grandmother, great-grandfather or great-grandmother, nor any other relation that I know of, or care a farthing for, has been in England these one hundred and fifty years; so that you see I have not one drop of blood in my veins but what is American.'

The prominent role Adams had played during the revolution meant that when George Washington became the nation's first President, Adams was elected as his Vice President. Had it been up to him, those titles would have been much grander: Adams argued that the leader should be 'His Majesty the President' or 'His High Mightiness, the President of the United States and Protector of their Liberties'. Thomas Jefferson called these suggestions 'superlatively ridiculous'. They, along with the fact that Adams was overweight, earned him the nickname 'His Rotundity'.

After Washington had served two terms, Adams bagged the top job in 1796, narrowly beating Jefferson, who became his Vice President. His time in office was marked by arguments, and Adams himself later admitted that he had been overly confrontational. 'I refused to suffer in silence. I sighed, sobbed, and groaned, and sometimes screeched and screamed. And I must confess to my shame and sorrow that I sometimes swore.' Which forms something of a contrast with the prayer he wrote for the Executive Mansion (which later became known as the White House). Washington had lived in New York and Philadelphia as President, but in 1800 Adams moved into the newly built residence. On the second day he wrote to his wife Abigail: 'I pray Heaven to bestow the best of blessings on this House, and all that shall hereafter inhabit it. May none but honest and wise men ever rule under this roof.' In 1945 Franklin D. Roosevelt had these words carved into the mantel in the State Dining Room.

In the bitterly fought election of 1800 Adams failed to secure a second term, being defeated by his own Vice President. So depressed was he (his alcoholic son Charles had recently died, and Adams missed his wife, who was living back in Massachusetts) that refused to attend his successor's inauguration (one of only four ex-Presidents ever to do so). He left the White House at 4 o'clock that morning. But years later the two men were reconciled, going on to swap many letters over a period of 14 years.

John Adams lived to see his son John Quincy Adams become the sixth President in 1825. He died the following year, on 4 July 1826, exactly 50 years to the day since the Declaration of Independence. It was 6.20 p.m. when he passed away, his final words including a statement of how glad he was that his longtime rival was still living: 'Thomas Jefferon survives.' Unknown to Adams, Jefferson had died that morning.

James Garfield: second US President to be assassinated

Unlike Abraham Lincoln, who was into his second term as President when he was assassinated, James A. Garfield served only four months in the White House before meeting the bullet with his name on it. Even though he clung to life for two months, he still died a few weeks short of his 50th birthday, making him one of only two Presidents not to reach that age. The other was John F. Kennedy.

From humble origins (he was the last President born in a log cabin), Garfield excelled at school. He could simultaneously write in Latin with one hand and Greek with the

other. He completed nine terms in the House of Representatives before becoming President on 4 March 1881 (and
remains the only sitting House member to take the White
House). From the start he was hounded by Charles Guiteau,
who had written a speech in support of Garfield during the
election campaign. Guiteau claimed this had been the de-
ciding factor in Garfield's victory, despite it being handed
out in written form rather than delivered as a speech, and
despite the fact that those copies contained several references
to Ulysses S. Grant rather than James A. Garfield. Grant had
been Garfield's predecessor as favourite for the Republican
nomination, and Guiteau's speech was originally written
about him. He missed some of the instances of Grant's name
when he went through the speech changing it.

Unsurprisingly Garfield disagreed with Guiteau's assess-
ment that he owed him something – a diplomatic posting,
maybe – and by May had to have Guiteau banned from
the White House waiting room. This would have come as
no surprise to Guiteau's family, who in 1875 had tried to
have him committed for insanity. Had they succeeded, the
nation's 20th President would have served a longer term:
Guiteau's resentment turned to rage, and he decided to
kill Garfield. He bought a revolver with an ivory handle,
on the grounds that it would look good when exhibited in
a museum after the assassination. The first time he fired it
the gun's kick nearly threw him off his feet. But he carried
on practising, and in June began following Garfield around
Washington.

Once, Guiteau trailed the President to the Baltimore
and Potomac Railroad station, but decided not to shoot
him then as Garfield's wife Lucretia, who had been in poor

health, was present and he didn't want to upset her. But on 2 July 1881 he returned to the station, from where – it had been announced in the newspapers – Garfield would be leaving for his summer vacation. When the President entered the waiting room, Guiteau fired at him from behind at point-blank range. Garfield cried: 'My God, what is that?' Guiteau shot him again, then tried to leave in a cab he had kept waiting outside the station. But a policeman intercepted him. 'I am a Stalwart of the Stalwarts!' shouted Guiteau, referring to an anti-Garfield faction in the Republican Party. 'I did it and I want to be arrested! Arthur is President now!'

But it would be a while before Vice President Chester Arthur took over. Garfield refused to die, spending several weeks in the White House under the care of doctors. Not very good care, it has to be said: one bullet had remained lodged in his body, and they probed for it with unsterilised fingers. One doctor even punctured Garfield's liver in the process, and infection set in. Alexander Graham Bell attended to try out a metal detector he had invented specifically to find the bullet. But the metal bed frame interfered with its operation, and a doctor insisted that Bell could only use it on Garfield's right side, where he believed the bullet was. It turned out to be on the left side. Bell maintained that, had he been allowed to use the detector in that region, he would have found it.

The President only met his Cabinet once, on 29 July, and even then they were under instructions from the doctors not to discuss anything distressing. Garfield's sole official act during this time was to sign a request for the extradition of a forger who had escaped to Canada. As the Washington summer grew hotter, fans were installed to blow air over a box of ice and towards the President. This early air conditioner lowered the temperature considerably, but Garfield's health continued to worsen. Despite a move to New Jersey to escape the capital's heat, he died on 19 September.

Guiteau's trial started in November. He insulted his own defence team, sought legal advice from spectators in the court, and spoke in long poems. He also sang 'John Brown's Body', as well as dictating his autobiography to the *New York Herald*. It ended with a lonely hearts appeal, Guiteau saying he would like to meet a Christian woman under the age of 30. He was found guilty in January 1882 and hanged in June. He danced his way up to the gallows, waved at the audience and shook hands with his executioner. As his last request he was allowed to recite a poem of his own composition called 'I Am Going to the Lordy', though he was not permitted an orchestra to accompany the performance, as he had wished. The noose was then fitted around Guiteau's neck, and he gave the agreed signal that he was ready to die: dropping the piece of paper on which the poem was written.

Despite the second assassination of a President, occupants of the White House still didn't receive Secret Service protection until 20 years later, after William McKinley had become the third President to be killed.

Jonathan Trumbull: second Speaker of the US House of Representatives

In 1791 Jonathan Trumbull took over as Speaker of the United States House of Representatives from Frederick Muhlenberg, the man who had suggested that the country's leader be called simply 'President', rather than 'His High Mightiness, the President of the United States and Protector of their Liberties'. The latter had been the suggestion of the second President, John Adams (see p. 70).

During the War of Independence Trumbull had served George Washington as his aide-de-camp. He was a native of Connecticut, and specifically the town of Lebanon. This settlement – the first in Connecticut to be named after somewhere in the Bible – was so called because of its cedar trees, which were said to be similar to the ones used to build King Solomon's temple.

Karl Dönitz: second leader of Nazi Germany

As the final days of World War II played themselves out, and Adolf Hitler contemplated the end of his life, he considered the question of who should take over as leader of Germany. Hermann Göring was commonly seen as his natural successor, but the Reichsmarschall had angered the Führer by openly asking him for the job. Similarly Heinrich Himmler – after swearing loyalty to Hitler the last time they ever met (20 April, Hitler's birthday) – had left Berlin to enter peace negotiations with the head of the Swedish Red Cross. When Hitler discovered this he was furious, and in his last will and testament he declared both Himmler and Göring to be traitors, expelling them from the Nazi Party.

So in the end the job went – under the terms of that same will – to Admiral Karl Dönitz, Commander-in-Chief of the German Navy. After Hitler's suicide on 30 April 1945, Dönitz appointed Count Ludwig Schwerin von Krosigk as

'Leading Minister', and the pair tried to form a government. They had to do this on the run, fleeing from Berlin to the town of Flensburg in the north of Germany. Knowing the military situation was hopeless, they concentrated their efforts on bringing the war to as swift an end as possible. Dönitz was worried about soldiers receiving brutal treatment from the Soviets, so tried wherever possible to ensure they surrendered to British or American forces instead. He specifically ordered his negotiators to spin out their peace talks with US General Dwight D. Eisenhower to allow more time for this to happen. Eventually Eisenhower demanded an end to the stalling, but Dönitz's efforts helped 1.8 million Germans avoid capture by the Soviets.

Dönitz also had to contend with Heinrich Himmler trying to wheedle himself back into favour. On the very first day after Hitler's death, Himmler had headed to Dönitz's office. 'At about midnight he arrived,' wrote the Admiral later, 'accompanied by six armed SS officers, and was received by my aide-de-camp, Walter Luedde-Neurath. I offered Himmler a chair and sat down at my desk, on which lay, hidden by some papers, a pistol with the safety catch off. I had never done anything of this sort in my life before, but I did not know what the outcome of this meeting might be.' He gave Himmler the telegram announcing his own appointment as Hitler's successor. 'As he read, an expression of astonishment, indeed of consternation, spread over his face. All hope seemed to collapse within him. He went very pale. Finally he stood up and bowed. "Allow me," he said, "to become the second man in your state." I replied that was out of the question and that there was no way I could make any use of his services. Thus advised, he left me at about one o'clock in the morning. The showdown had taken place without force, and I felt relieved.'

Dönitz's brief reign as the second – and final – leader of Nazi Germany came to an end on 23 May, when he was arrested by Squadron Leader Mark Hobden of the RAF. His Kriegsmarine (Nazi Navy) flag was taken, and now resides at the RAF Regiment Heritage Centre at Honington in Suffolk. His ceremonial baton is in Shrewsbury Castle, as part of the museum of the King's Shopshire Light Infantry, who were also involved in the surrender of senior members of Dönitz's government. It was an inauspicious end to a military career that had begun before World War I, when Dönitz joined the navy. He had been captured in that conflict too, and held in a prisoner-of-war camp near Sheffield. Fearful that as the captain of a U-boat he might be prosecuted for war crimes, he pretended to be mentally ill. This got him transferred to a hospital in Manchester, and in 1920 he returned to Germany.

Dönitz went on to be a keen supporter of Hitler. However, during World War II his assiduous monitoring of boats while in charge of the navy actually hindered rather than helped: contacting them over 70 times a day meant that British codebreakers had all the more ammunition with which to complete their work. And after the war Dönitz was astounded to be charged with war crimes, on the grounds that he had been head of state. 'How can a foreign court try a sovereign government of another country? Could we have tried your President Franklin Delano Roosevelt . . . or Winston Churchill?' The authorities at Nuremberg disagreed, and Dönitz was sentenced to ten years in Spandau Prison. He remained the only ex-head of state to be convicted by an international tribunal until 2012, when Liberia's Charles

Taylor gained his own entry in the 'seconds' hall of fame.

On his release Dönitz argued with the West German government about his pension. They wanted to pay him only as a captain, because all his promotions above that level had been made due to Hitler liking him, rather than on genuine merit. Dönitz took them to court and won, receiving a full admiral's pension for the rest of his life. He wrote a book called *Ten Years and Twenty Days* – the former was the period he'd spent as a U-boat commander, the latter that as leader of Germany.

He died of a heart attack on Christmas Eve 1980.

Tiberius: second Roman Emperor

'The gloomiest of men' might not be the most flattering way to be remembered, but thanks to the Roman historian Pliny the Elder, who called Tiberius *tristissimus hominum*, it's the verdict Rome's second Emperor is lumbered with.

The first Emperor is taken to be Augustus, his predecessor Julius Caesar being seen as the last Roman dictator. Augustus died in AD 14, and was succeeded as Princeps (the Roman term for Emperor – it literally means 'first citizen') by his stepson Tiberius. At first Tiberius fared well, continuing the previous success which had included helping to expand the empire into what is now part of Germany. In 15 BC he had discovered the sources of the Danube, Europe's second-longest river (see 'Danube', p. 121).

But partly due to the death of his own son in AD 23, Tiberius lost enthusiasm for his role. He retired to the island of Capri, leaving duties in Rome to his Praetorian prefects (chief ministers of state) Sejanus and, later, Macro. The Roman historian Suetonius writes of Tiberius indulging in orgies and paedophilia on Capri, but later historians are more favourable to him.

Tiberius died in AD 37. His will made his grandson Gemellus joint heir along with Gaius, son of the general Germanicus. But after assuming the role of Emperor Gaius voided the will and had Gemellus executed. He continued to reign in the same fashion, known by his more famous nickname: Caligula.

Arthur Wellesley: 2nd Duke of Wellington

Arthur Wellesley's military career saw him become a captain in the Royal Horse Guards, a lieutenant-colonel in the Victoria (Middlesex) Rifle Volunteer Corps and, in 1854, a major-general. His political career included membership of the Privy Council, spells as MP for Aldeburgh and Norwich, and service as Master of the Horse in the governments of Lord Aberdeen and Lord Palmerston. He was also a Knight of the Garter. But from his earliest days, Wellesley realised that he would be known for one thing and one thing only: he was the son of the 1st Duke of Wellington. 'Imagine what it will be,' he once said, 'when the Duke of Wellington is announced, and only I walk in the room.'

It can't have been easy, living in the shadow of a father who had beaten Napoleon and served as Prime Minister. Wellesley contented himself with friendships, including one with Thomas Raikes, a City financier and gambler whose membership of several Pall Mall clubs earned him the nickname 'Apollo', because he 'rose in the east and set in the west'. And Wellesley can't have known it at the time, but during their childhood the Brontë sisters (a decade or so younger than him) played games about the colonisation of Africa that featured him, his brother and his father. They also wrote stories based on the games, in which Wellesley is a heroic figure, sometimes known as the Duke of Zamorna, later as the Emperor Adrian of Angria. He is also said to have inspired the character of Edward Rochester in Charlotte Brontë's *Jane Eyre*.

Even Wellesley's death was less than glamorous: instead of breathing his last at Apsley House (the family's London home) or Stratfield Saye (their Hampshire estate), in 1884 he collapsed and died at Brighton train station. Transport also features in another of his connections: in 1863, by now the Duke of Wellington (his father had died in 1852), he inherited the extra title of Earl of Mornington. The preceding Earl had been his cousin William Pole-Tylney-Long-Wellesley, but a previous holder of the title had been his uncle (the 1st Duke's brother). It was after this Earl that Mornington Crescent in London was named. The street later bequeathed its name to a Tube station, which in turn inspired a Radio 4 institution.

St Linus: second Pope

St Peter, having been appointed by Jesus as the head of what we now call the Roman Catholic Church, is deemed by the religion to be the first Pope (though he never used that title, or its allied one, 'Vicar of Christ'). On his death (around AD 67) he was succeeded by St Linus.

Linus had been born c.AD 10 in Volterra, Tuscany. He served as Pope until his death in c.AD 76. His only known instruction was that women should cover their heads in church. This followed the teaching in St Paul's first letter to the Corinthians, that 'man . . . is the image and glory of God, but woman is the glory of man'. Accordingly 'any man who prays or prophesies with his head covered brings shame upon his head', but 'any woman who prays or prophesies with her head unveiled brings shame upon her head'.

It's not known for sure how Linus died, though some believe he was martyred for his Christian beliefs by the Romans. If so he would have followed his predecessor, who chose to be crucified upside down, saying he was unworthy to die the same way as Christ. This is why a St Peter's cross is a normal crucifix inverted.

The first five Popes were Peter, Linus, Anacletus, Clement and Evaristus. Catholic students remember them with the mnemonic 'PLACE'.

Two Penny Blue: the world's second official postage stamp

The Two Penny Blue should have appeared on the same day (1 May 1840) as the more famous Penny Black, but it didn't actually go on sale until 6 May. It was exactly the same as the other stamp, except for the two differences you'd expect from its name: it was blue rather than black, and cost twice as much. This was because it was valid for a letter weighing up to an ounce – the Penny Black only covered you for half an ounce.

Both stamps were printed by Perkins, Bacon and Co. The second name belonged to Joshua Butters Bacon, the former to his father-in-law and founder of the firm, Jacob Perkins. An American inventor, Perkins had developed the rose engine which allowed the printing of the complicated anti-forgery patterns on both stamps. His other work included an early refrigerator, a machine for making nails and a steam-powered automatic gun that could fire 1,000 rounds per minute. It was rejected by the Duke of Wellington for being 'too destructive'.

The King's School, Rochester: second-oldest continuously operating school in the world

Seven years and 25 miles are all that separate this second from its first. Even their names are almost the same. King's School, Canterbury, was founded in AD 597, while its namesake down the A2 in Rochester first called the register in AD 604. Its foundation occurred at the same time as the Kent town's cathedral. When Henry VIII dissolved Rochester's monastery in 1541 he refounded the school.

Its administrative offices are situated in Satis House, originally built for Richard Watts, a Rochester businessman who served as the town's MP in the 16th century. The unusual name arose when Elizabeth I stayed there in 1573 – as she was leaving, Watts asked the queen whether she had enjoyed her stay, and she replied: '*Satis*' (Latin for 'enough'). Satis House was used by Charles Dickens as the home of Miss Havisham in *Great Expectations*. Havisham's adopted daughter Estella explains the story to Pip, who says that 'Enough House' is a 'curious name'. She points out that 'it meant more than it said. It meant, when it was given, that whoever had this house, could want nothing else. They must have been easily satisfied in those days, I should think.'

Richard Watts died in 1579. His will began: 'First I bequeath my Soule unto the Holy Trinity', and went on to specify arrangements for his funeral. These included the stipulation that every 'poore Body' attending the service would receive 'One penney in bread and One penny in money'. He set aside £5 for this, implying an expected 600 attendees.

The café and tuck shop at King's are located in a building called Bob Doubles. This wasn't the name of an old boy – it's a series of changes used in bell-ringing. One old Roffensian who *is* commemorated at the school is John Storrs, who went on to be Dean of Rochester between 1913 and 1928, and who gave his surname to one of the school's five houses (the groups into which pupils are separated for sporting and other activities). Storrs had six children. The eldest, Ronald, worked for the Foreign Office, and was described by T.E. Lawrence in *Seven Pillars of Wisdom* as 'the most brilliant Englishman in the Near East' (Storrs later acted as a pallbearer at Lawrence's funeral). The second eldest, Francis, died the day before the end of World War I; John Storrs received the telegram telling him of his son's death as he was on his way to Rochester Cathedral to preach at the service of thanksgiving for the war's conclusion. Francis had died in Chelsea of Spanish flu, but had seen active service during the conflict. In fact in May 1917 he lost his two front teeth, though the blame lay firmly with Storrs himself – the damage was caused by the recoil from a three-pounder gun he was test-firing. Storrs had ignored a warning to remove his pipe.

The houses in the pre-prep school at King's are called Tigers, Hippos, Giraffes and Zebras. The last of these used to be called Snakes but some of the children found that too frightening.

Old Roffensians who have achieved fame in recent years include the Conservative MP John Selwyn Gummer, whose son Ben also became a Tory MP but whose daughter Cordelia is probably still more famous for having been offered a burger by her father during the BSE crisis – she refused it. There is also the ex-Radio 1 DJ commemorated in the Cockney rhyming slang phrase 'it's all gone Pete Tong' (wrong).

Cambridge University: second-oldest university in Britain

No one knows exactly when Oxford University was founded: it's believed to have been at some point between 1096 and 1167. But there's no doubt that Cambridge came later – it was only founded because scholars from Oxford needed a new home. Two of their colleagues had been hanged by the town's authorities for their role in the death of a woman. Normally the Church would have intervened and pardoned the scholars. In protest at this not happening, the remaining academics left Oxford. Some of them travelled to Cambridge and established the new university in 1209. (It thus became the second in Britain, and third in the world – the University of Bologna dates from 1088.)

Since then Oxford and Cambridge have grown to form twin pillars of the British establishment. In one episode of *Yes, Minister* Sir Humphrey Appleby lists the 'important things of life' as 'the opera, Radio 3, the countryside, the law, the universities . . . both of them'. But as so often in life, those closest to you are the ones with whom you fight most fiercely: the rivalry between Oxford and Cambridge is legendary. The second-oldest university can claim more Nobel Prize winners (89 to Oxford's 58), but when it comes to British prime ministers Oxford has had as many from one college (Christ Church) as Cambridge has had in total (14 – Oxford's overall score is 27). Both universities have the right to print and distribute the King James Bible and Book of Common Prayer in England, Wales and Northern Ireland (in Scotland that right is reserved for a body known as the Bible Board), though Cambridge University Press can claim to be older, and indeed is the oldest publishing house in the world, having been granted its letters patent by Henry VIII in 1534. The first University Printer was Thomas Thomas, proving that through the ages there have always been parents who simply should not be allowed to name their children. In the mid-18th century the Printer was John Baskerville, designer of the typeface we still use today. CUP has its own shop at 1 Trinity Street: books have been sold on this site since at least 1581 (possibly even earlier), making it the oldest bookshop site in Britain.

Sidney Sussex College has the full title 'the College of the Lady Frances Sidney Sussex', she being the countess – and former Lady of the Bedchamber to Elizabeth I – who left £5,000 in her will to found it. But of course titles get shortened, so now everyone thinks it was founded by a man. Either way, the college is surely the only organisation in the world to own both a stick of seaside rock from Cleethorpes and the skull of an English ruler. The rock is kept in the college archives to denote the link with the Lincolnshire town developed on land owned by the college, while the skull is that of Oliver Cromwell. When Charles II regained the throne in 1660 he decided to put Cromwell on trial for treason. A slight complication was that Cromwell had died in 1658, but the King wasn't going to let that deter him – he had the body dug up and taken to the Old Bailey, where Cromwell was (perhaps unsurprisingly) found guilty. His corpse was beheaded, and the treasonous bonce placed on a spike outside Westminster Hall. It stayed there for over 20 years, until in 1685 a storm blew it to the ground. After that the skull passed between private owners for three centuries. Finally, in 1960, it was acquired by Sidney Sussex, the college Cromwell had himself attended. Such is his controversial reputation even today that the authorities had to bury it in a secret location within the college grounds to keep it safe. A more recent student at Sidney Sussex was *Countdown*'s mathematical whizz Carol Vorderman, who scored a third in all three of her years there, so earning membership of the 'Nines Club'.

Low grades at Cambridge are nothing new: the university is the home of the wooden spoon, originally awarded to the student who achieved the lowest mark in the Mathematical Tripos without actually failing. The spoons could be up to 5 feet long, and were dangled in front of the recipient from the upstairs balcony of Senate House as he was awarded his degree: this practice was eventually banned in 1875. The last wooden spoon was presented in 1909, to Cuthbert Lempriere Holthouse. It was inscribed with a Greek epigram which translates as:

In Honours Mathematical,
This is the very last of all
The Wooden Spoons which you see here;
O you who see it, shed a tear.

Cambridge's links with politics don't stop at its 14 prime ministers – there's also the house they inhabit. Downing College was founded with money left by Sir George Downing, who built the famous London street. When Number 10 was refurbished in the 1960s one of its old doors was taken to Cambridge and is now in use in the college. And, like Oxford and London universities, Cambridge was until 1950 a constituency in the UK Parliament – not a geographical one, rather a seat (in fact two seats) elected by graduates of the university. (They also had their conventional vote wherever they lived, so actually got to cast two ballots in each election.) William Pitt the Younger and Lord Palmerston both served as MPs for Cambridge University.

When Lord Byron went up to Trinity College he was prevented by the authorities from keeping his beloved dog Boatswain. Infuriated, the poet examined the rule book and found that although it forbade dogs and cats, there was nothing about bears. So he acquired one and kept that instead. 'When I brought him here,' he wrote to a friend, 'they asked me what I meant to do with him, and my reply was, "He should sit for a fellowship."' Other undergraduates contented themselves with games of football: the rules first used in 1848 for a game on Parker's Piece (the park in the middle of Cambridge) were the basis for the game as established by the Football Association in 1863.

But the university's most unusual pastime is Cambridge Night Climbing. This tradition sees undergraduates scaling seemingly unclimbable buildings in the hours of darkness, leaving behind various objects as proof of their success. In 1958, for instance, some engineering students from Gonville and Caius College baffled everyone by somehow lifting an Austin Seven van onto the roof of Senate House. It took the authorities a week to get it back down. In another stunt someone managed to scale the walls of King's College Chapel and leave a traffic cone on one of the spires. The next morning the college began erecting scaffolding to retrieve the cone, but by the end of the day the job hadn't been finished. That night the pranksters went back up and moved the cone to the opposite end of the building, so rendering the half-built scaffolding useless.

Dueller's assistant: second by name . . .

When two people agree to settle their differences by a duel, their assistants are called 'seconds'. Different sets of rules have governed such events down the centuries, each known as a 'Code Duello'. The one adopted in Ireland in 1777 included a proviso (rule 25) for when seconds themselves disagreed and had their own duel. The rule stated that this must happen at the same time as, and at right angles to, the principals.

In 1842, before he was President of the US, Abraham Lincoln arranged to fight a duel with the politician James Shields. Lincoln had written a letter to an Illinois newspaper making fun of Shields (the State Auditor), who challenged Lincoln to a duel. Knowing that his opponent was an excellent shot, Lincoln chose swords as the weapons, and met Shields on Bloody Island, which lay outside the jurisdiction of Illinois (where duelling was illegal). As they were about to start, Lincoln demonstrated his longer reach by cutting a branch near Shields's head. The two seconds intervened and persuaded the two principals to abandon the duel.

In Kentucky politicians taking the oath of office have to swear that they have not fought a duel or acted as a second.

Grocers' Company: second most important livery company

The livery companies of the City of London are bodies which represent various trades and professions. By 1515 there were 48 of them, and they decided to rank themselves according to economic and political standing. Top spot went to the Mercers (another word for 'merchant'). In second place were the Grocers. The list is still in place today: companies formed since 1515 are added in order of creation. So at 105 is the Worshipful Company of Management Consultants, followed by the Worshipful Companies of International Bankers, Tax Advisers, Security Professionals and Educators, with the Worshipful Company of Arts Scholars bringing up the rear at position 110.

The Grocers' Company was founded in 1345, growing out

of the older Guild of Pepperers. Its responsibilities included the setting of weights and measures, as well as maintaining purity standards for spices. This explains the camel in its coat of arms (the animal was used in spice transportation). The company also included London's pharmacists, until they left in 1617 to form the Worshipful Society of Apothecaries.

Under its motto 'God Grant Grace', the company (like many others) functions these days as a charitable institution. It is responsible for Oundle School in Northamptonshire, founded in 1556 by Sir William Laxton, eight times Master of the company. This explains the camel on the school's badge. Old boys range from the scientist Richard Dawkins to Bruce Dickinson of Iron Maiden. The company also built a village in Northern Ireland. It is now known as Eglinton, having seen fit to change from the original name of Muff.

Some claim that the Grocers were in fact top of the original livery rankings, but were made to swap places with the Mercers after their camel farted in Elizabeth I's face. It wouldn't have been the only controversy surrounding the list. The Company of Watermen and Lightermen, who control the boats on the River Thames, are still not deemed to be a full livery company because of their behaviour after the Great Fire of London: they insisted on charging those who fled across the river to escape the blaze. And to this day, over four centuries after the list was drawn up, the Merchant Taylors and the Skinners cannot agree who should be in sixth and seventh places – so they continue to alternate every year. This is the origin of the phrase 'at sixes and sevens'.

COUNTRIES

◆

Monaco: second-smallest country in the world

Until 2005 Monaco was breathing slightly harder down Vatican City's neck in the fight to be the world's smallest country. The enclave in Rome takes up 0.17 square miles, while Monaco measured 0.76. Then some land was reclaimed from the sea, taking Monaco up to a positively expansive 0.78 square miles, though this is still only half the size of New York's Central Park. And Monaco remains the smallest country with a coastline.

It is ruled by the Grimaldi family, and has been since 1297, when François Grimaldi led the small army that conquered it (to this day the Grimaldi coat of arms bears the image of monks carrying swords). They are the oldest ruling family in Europe. Until 2002 ownership of the country would have passed to France if the Grimaldi line had died out – but now a treaty dictates that even then Monaco would remain an independent nation.

Its population of 38,400 makes Monaco the most densely populated country on Earth (49,230 people per square mile). Someone born there is 'Monegasque', while someone born elsewhere but resident in the country is a 'Monacan'.

The latter make up about 80 per cent of the population, and their wealth gives Monaco the third-highest GDP per capita in the world, behind only Liechtenstein (the country with more companies than people) and Qatar.

Some of this wealth is gambled in the famous casino at Monte Carlo (which Monegasques are not allowed to enter). The casino was closed for a day in 1958 to celebrate the birth of Caroline, the first child of Prince Rainier III and his wife Grace Kelly. (Their second child, Albert, is now Monaco's ruler.) The song 'The Man Who Broke the Bank at Monte Carlo' was inspired by Charles Wells, who over two visits in 1891 turned £4,000 into £60,000 (worth over £6m today). Several times he cleaned out the reserves of the table on which he was playing: this was known as 'breaking the bank', and was marked by a black cloth being laid over the table while more funds were brought from the casino's vaults. Wells was a convicted fraudster, so there is some speculation about whether his winnings were achieved fairly.

The Monaco marathon is the only one in the world to pass through three countries (the home country, France and Italy), while the Grand Prix held there every year is famed for its tight, twisting course. Nelson Piquet compared it to 'riding a bicycle around your living room'. The day after Ayrton Senna's victory in the 1987 race the driver was stopped for riding a motorcycle without wearing a helmet. When the police realised who he was, they let him go. Monaco is the only Grand Prix not to use a podium – the presentation ceremony is held on the steps of the royal box.

Monaco's football team play in the French league. Its stadium, the Stade Louis II, can hold over half of Monaco's population.

Canada: second-largest country in the world

'Toronto,' said Peter Ustinov, 'is New York run by the Swiss.' And Canadian tourists the world over get annoyed at being asked which part of America they're from. But in terms of area the country putting Canada in the shade isn't the USA (that comes third) – it's Russia. Canada's 3.5 million square miles are dwarfed by Russia's 6.6 million – even the difference between them would rank as the seventh-largest country in the world.

But does Russia have over 60 per cent of the world's lakes? No: that's Canada. The country even has the world's largest lake within an island within a lake. Lake Manitou has an island in it (the planet's largest lake island, naturally), and within *that* there is a lake. Until recently Canada was also home to the largest French-speaking city other than Paris. Montreal has now slipped to fourth in the list, though thanks mainly to African cities you get to number nine before you find another one in France (Lyon).

The somewhat staid image you might get from the Ustinov quote isn't entirely without foundation. In the town of Petrolia, Ontario, it is illegal to whistle. Officials say this is merely to limit excessive noise at night, but Article 3, 772.3.6 on the town's website states: 'Yelling, shouting, hooting, whistling or singing is prohibited at all times.' And in Souris, Prince Edward Island, it is illegal for anyone living on a corner lot to build a snowman taller than 30 inches. Petrolia's name honours its oil industry, by the way. There's plenty of oil in Canada – the US imports more from its neighbour than from Saudi Arabia.

Perhaps to try and counter Canada's overly law-abiding

impression, Steve McVittie, a foodstore owner in Vancouver, helps Americans get round their country's ban on haggis. The traditional Scottish delicacy (containing sheep's lung, heart and liver) is outlawed in the US because officials deem it unfit for human consumption. But Scots working in the state of Washington refuse to be denied their Burns Night fare: they make round trips of up to 300 miles to McVittie's store to buy a haggis, supplied to McVittie by a butcher in the same city. (The butcher's identity remains a secret.) They then smuggle the contraband back home, over part of the world's longest border (5,525 miles). The world's second-longest is that between Russia and Kazakhstan (4,254 miles). Canada also beats the world in the length of its coastline (125,566 miles) – runner-up is Indonesia, whose more than 17,000 islands muster 33,998 miles of coastline between them.

Canada can do small as well. In Rodney, Ontario, you'll find the world's tiniest prison. The Coby Jail dates from 1884, measures 270 square feet and boasts just two cells. Its 2-foot-thick limestone walls were mined from the local quarry, though they didn't stop an inmate called Lee from escaping – the constable who found him sitting outside the prison could find no damage to the lock or the door. The explanation? The man who built the jail, Albert Ryckman, put some of the bricks in place without any mortar, so he could remove them should he ever find himself a captive of his own structure. Which he did. Several times.

The board game Trivial Pursuit was invented in Canada. Scott Abbott and Chris Haney of Montreal were playing Scrabble one day in 1979 when they found that some of the pieces were missing. So they decided to invent their own game. Its eventual success was so great that they once attracted a $300m lawsuit. An author claimed that the game's answer to the question of Lieutenant Columbo's first name (Philip) was actually a deliberate mistake inserted into one of his books to trap people stealing his material. The makers of Trivial Pursuit admitted that they had used the author's books as sources, but claimed that facts are not protected by copyright. The court ruled in their favour. For the record: Columbo's name is never officially revealed in the credits or dialogue of the programme, though glimpses of his badge do sometimes reveal it as 'Frank'.

The world's two largest countries came to blows in 1987, during their match at the World Junior Ice Hockey Championships in Czechoslovakia (though Russia was then of course part of the Soviet Union). Some blamed the inexperienced Norwegian referee, but the direct cause of the melee was a collision between the Soviet Union's Sergei Shesterikov and Canada's Everett Sanipass. Four Soviet players left the bench to join in the brawl, or rather brawls (there were at least a dozen separate fights all over the ice). The violence continued for 20 minutes, at which point the authorities sought to achieve peace by turning off the arena lights. The players simply continued fighting in the dark.

Llanfairpwllgwyngyllgogerychwyrndrobwllllantysili-ogogogoch: second-longest place name in the world

As publicity stunts go, this one is a winner. Over a century and a half since the Welsh village created its 58-letter name to attract tourists, we're still talking about it. The moniker was originally chosen to gain the title of 'longest train station name in Britain', and the platform sign now includes a pronunciation guide: 'Llan-vire-pooll-guin-gill-go-ger-u-queern-drob-ooll-llandus-ilio-gogo-goch'. The meaning is: 'Saint Mary's Church in a hollow of white hazel near the swirling whirlpool of the Church of Saint Tysilio with a red cave.'

Stephen Sondheim worked the name into the lyrics of his song 'The Boy From . . .', a parody of 'The Girl From Ipanema'. In the film *Barbarella* it is the password for the headquarters of the revolutionary Dildano. (The same film's villain Durand Durand gave Duran Duran their name.) In *The Road to Hong Kong* a doctor played by Peter Sellers asks Bob Hope to say it (instead of 'ahh') as he examines him. And in 1979 Roger Squires, crossword compiler for the *Telford and Wrekin News*, managed to work it into one of his puzzles.

In 1915 Llanfair PG (as it is commonly known) hosted the first-ever Women's Institute meeting in Britain. The movement (which had started in Canada) encouraged women to become more involved in food production while their men were away fighting in World War I. The actress Naomi Watts spent part of her childhood there, and once delighted a US chat-show audience by pronouncing the village's name in full. Channel 4's weatherman Liam Dutton also accomplished the feat during a 2015 forecast, the YouTube video of which has clocked up over 15 million views.

Someone else who can pronounce the world's longest place name is Martina Navratilova. Not because the tennis star grew up there – simply because, aged ten, on a rainy day in her native Czechoslovakia, she learned to say:

Taumatawhakatangihangakoauauotamateaturipukakapik-
imaungahoronukupokaiwhenuakitanatahu. Which came
in handy when she visited the hill in New Zealand, and
was able to thank the local people for their hospitality by
reciting the name. It means 'the summit where Tamatea,
the man with the big knees, the climber of mountains, the
land-swallower who travelled about, played his nose flute to
his loved one'.

The second-longest place name in Britain is Cottons-
hopeburnfoot, a hamlet in Northumberland. It derives from
the burn (small river) called Cottonshope, which meets the
River Rede there. Some people spell it Cottonshopeburn
Foot, which would lose it the title of 'longest place name in
England'. Though if the aim is (like Llanfair PG) to attract
tourists, the area needn't worry – the title then passes to
Blakehopeburnhaugh, a mile down the road.

Nauru: second-smallest population in the world

In 1798, a British navigator sailing from New Zealand to
the China Seas passed an 8-square-mile speck in the ocean.
Saying what he saw, he named it 'Pleasant Island'. Since
then Nauru, to use its modern title, has had a somewhat
chequered history.

The name is said to derive from the native word meaning
'I go to the beach'. And certainly its idyllic Pacific setting,
1,800 miles north-east of Australia, explains why Micrones-
ians and Polynesians settled there over 3,000 years ago. They
eventually organised into 12 clans, which is why the star
on Nauru's modern flag has that number of points. In the

mid-19th century the population began to be augmented by deserters from passing European ships. They paid for food from the islanders with wine and guns. Never a wise mix, and in 1878 Nauru began a decade-long tribal war.

In 1919 Brigadier-General Thomas Griffiths, the island's Australian administrator, declared after a meeting with local chiefs that the native population was dangerously low, and that if Nauruans wanted to survive as a race they needed to number at least 1,500. When that figure was reached, he said, a public holiday would be declared, and celebrated every year thereafter. The baby who achieved the magic number would be the 'Angam baby' (from the word for 'to have reached a set goal'), and would be given gifts. Things got off to a bad start with the 1920 influenza epidemic that wiped out nearly one in five Nauruans, but eventually in 1932 Eidegenegen Eidagaruwo became the Angam baby. Her birthday, 26 October, continues to be celebrated. Not that she celebrated many of them herself. During World War II, when the island was occupied by Japan, Eidegenegen and 1,200 other Nauruans were evacuated to nearby Truk. There she died, as did many of the others, from malnutrition.

Nauru gained its independence in 1968, led by President Hammer DeRoburt. This was a successful period for the island, due to the phosphate reserves that had been discovered. Indeed for a while it enjoyed the highest per-capita income in the world. But then the reserves ran out. Nauru tried to recover its standard of living by becoming a tax haven and money-laundering centre, but international authorities soon put a stop to that. An unhappy legacy of the years of plenty, during which people abandoned their traditional lifestyle of fishing and gardening, is that Nauru's population is the fattest of any nation on Earth: 97 per cent of men and 93 per cent of women are overweight or obese. It also has the highest level of type 2 diabetes, over 40 per cent of the population suffering from the condition.

The country has become dependent on aid, as well as the income derived from the Australian government for housing the controversial detention centre to which would-be asylum-seekers are sent. As of July 2016 the population had dwindled to just 9,591, the only four-digit figure for any sovereign state. (Vatican City houses about 800 people.) Nauru's population is slightly lower than that of Diss in Norfolk.

Delaware: second-smallest US state

As if Rhode Island's 1,214 square miles wasn't annoying enough (Delaware comes in at 1,982 square miles), the smallest state also has the longest name, being known officially as 'State of Rhode Island and Providence Plantations'. But Delaware doesn't mind, knowing that it has many points of interest of its own. Even its name has a tale to tell. It is taken from that of the Delaware River, which in turn is derived from Baron De La Warr, or Thomas West, as he was known to his friends. He was the Englishman who acted as Governor of the colony of Virginia.

Delaware is known as the 'First State', as in 1787 it ratified the US Constitution before any of the others. Its earliest settlement was Lewes, named after the town in England, and – also like its namesake – situated in the county of Sussex. Delaware's other counties are New Castle and Kent. This total of three is the lowest of any US state. Delaware also has (together with Pennsylvania) the only circular section of boundary in the US – the arc that separates them is known as the Twelve Mile Circle, being centred that distance from the cupola of the courthouse in the city of New Castle. (The only state without any straight lines in its border, meanwhile, remains Hawaii.)

New York might think it has bragging rights in the song stakes, but a song called 'Delaware' got to number three in the UK charts in 1960. The lyrics are all puns on the names of US states, beginning with 'What did Della wear?', to which the answer is 'A brand New Jersey'. Delaware was also the birthplace of nylon: DuPont began production of the material at their Seaford factory in 1939. And the annual chicken festival in Delmarva sees nearly 3 tons of the meat cooked each year. The festival gave rise to the world's largest frying pan – 10 feet in diameter and with an 8-foot handle, it weighed 650 pounds and could hold 800 chicken quarters.

But for an even greater food extreme, Delaware offers the world championship of 'Punkin Chunkin', the sport in which competitors hurl a pumpkin as far as they can. The devices they use have become so technically advanced that the record currently stands at 4,694.68 feet, or not far short of a mile. It is not clear, however, when anyone will get a chance to beat that: the event's future is uncertain after the 2017 championship was cancelled. This was because of a lawsuit relating to an injury suffered at the 2016 championship.

Texas: second-largest US state

People who regularly host quizzes will tell you that 'Which is the smallest country/state' questions always elicit the enquiry, 'Do you mean by area or population?' It's a fair point: Delaware, for instance, is only the second-smallest US state by area – by population the title goes to Vermont. But when it comes to the second-largest US state, Texas has both categories in the bag. Its area (268,596 square miles) is beaten only by Alaska (665,384), while its population (27,862,596) comes second to that of California (39,250,017). Neither winner is that surprising: California has more residents than the 21 least populous states combined, while if Alaska was a country it would be the 17th-biggest in the world. America's wide-open spaces are very wide indeed: 11 of the 50 states are bigger than the UK.

Texas's capital of Austin has its own 'second' credentials – only Phoenix in Arizona is a more populous state capital. Houston is the fourth most populous city in the US (after New York, Los Angeles and Chicago). Historically Texas built its economic strength on cattle, cotton and timber, but in the 20th century oil became king. So much so that if Texas was a country, it would have the tenth-largest economy in the world. Texas prides itself on standing alone, and until 1845, when it became the 28th state of the union, it was an independent republic. To this day it has a single five-pointed star on its flag, giving rise to the nickname 'the Lone Star State'. The slogan 'Don't Mess with Texas', however, is less scary than it might sound – it dates from an anti-litter campaign of the 1980s.

Third Street: second most common street name in the US

It's as delightfully perverse as the famous Abbott and Costello 'Who's on first?' sketch: first place on the list of most common US street names goes to Second, while second place is occupied by Third. Coming third is First.

There are 10,131 thoroughfares called Third Street, compared to 10,866 called Second Street. The name First Street appears 9,898 times, ahead of the 9,190 Fourth Streets, which makes that the only 'logical' name on the whole list. (Elsewhere Fifth is sixth, Sixth is eighth, Seventh is tenth and Eighth is fourteenth.) The explanation is that the 'major' street in a town or city is often called Main rather than First. If you combined these two labels they would indeed top the chart.

For the record: in the Abbott and Costello sketch, second base is occupied by 'What'.

CREDITS

Independent Television in Britain by Paul Bonner with Lesley Aston (Palgrave Macmillan 2003)

Nineteen Eighty-Four by George Orwell (Copyright © George Orwell, 1949)
Reprinted by permission of Bill Hamilton as the Literary Executor of the Estate of the Late Sonia Brownell Orwell.

Tolstoy's Bicycle by Jeremy Baker (Sphere Books, 1983)

Night Mail by W.H. Auden, 1936

Theme from 'Shaft' – Isaac Hayes (Universal Music Publishing Group)

Fairytale of New York – Jem Finer and Shane Patrick Lysaght MacGowan (Warner/Chappell Music Inc., Universal Music Publishing Group)

Delaware – Irving Gordon (Sony/ATV Music Publishing)

ACKNOWLEDGEMENTS

Many thanks as ever to Alan Samson, Lucinda McNeile, Simon Wright and everyone at Orion. Also to Martin Stubbs, Sam Beven, Charlotte Bishop and Seth Philbedge for their help with research. Thanks too to Special Agent Charlie Viney. And, of course, to Jo and Barney.

INDEX

INDEX